DATE DUE

POCAHONTAS

NORTH AMERICAN INDIANS OF ACHIEVEMENT

POCAHONTAS
Powhatan Peacemaker

▼▼▼

Anne Holler

Senior Consulting Editor
W. David Baird
Howard A. White Professor of History
Pepperdine University

CHELSEA HOUSE PUBLISHERS

New York   Philadelphia

FRONTISPIECE   A 19th-century painting of Pocahontas and her son, Thomas Rolfe. The portrait once hung in Heacham Hall, the ancestral home of Pocahontas's English husband.

ON THE COVER   A portrait of Pocahontas, based on an engraving by Dutch artist Simon van de Pass. Van de Pass's image is the only depiction of Pocahontas known to have been made during her life.

Chelsea House Publishers
EDITOR-IN-CHIEF   Richard S. Papale
MANAGING EDITOR   Karyn Gullen Browne
COPY CHIEF   Philip Koslow
PICTURE EDITOR   Adrian G. Allen
ART DIRECTOR   Nora Wertz
MANUFACTURING DIRECTOR   Gerald Levine
SYSTEMS MANAGER   Lindsey Ottman
PRODUCTION MANAGER   Joseph Romano
PRODUCTION COORDINATOR   Marie Claire Cebrián-Ume

North American Indians of Achievement
SENIOR EDITOR   Liz Sonneborn

Staff for POCAHONTAS
COPY EDITOR   Danielle Janusz
EDITORIAL ASSISTANT   Nicole Greenblatt
DESIGNER   Debora Smith
PICTURE RESEARCHER   Alan Gottlieb
COVER ILLUSTRATION   Shelley Pritchett

Printed and bound in Mexico.

First Printing

1   3   5   7   9   8   6   4   2

Library of Congress Cataloging-in-Publication Data

Holler, Anne.
Pocahontas: Powhatan Peacemaker/by Anne Holler
    p. cm.—(North American Indians of achievement)
Includes bibliographical references and index.
Summary: Discusses the life and times of Pocahontas and her role as peacemaker between the Powhatan tribes and the English settlers of Jamestown.
ISBN 0-7910-1705-2
0-7910-1952-7 (pbk.)
1. Pocahontas. d. 1617—Juvenile literature. 2. Powhatan, ca. 1550–1618—Juvenile literature. 3. Powhatan Indians—Biography—Juvenile literature. 4. Powhatan Indians—History—Juvenile literature. [1. Pocahontas, d. 1617. 2. Powhatan, ca. 1550–1618 3. Powhatan Indians—Biography. 4. Indians of North America—Biography.]
I. Title. II. Series.
E99.P85P5716 1993   91-9946
975'.5'01'092—dc20   CIP
[B]   AC

CONTENTS

NORTH AMERICAN INDIANS OF ACHIEVEMENT

BLACK HAWK
Sac Rebel

JOSEPH BRANT
Mohawk Chief

COCHISE
Apache Chief

CRAZY HORSE
Sioux War Chief

CHIEF GALL
Sioux War Chief

GERONIMO
Apache Warrior

HIAWATHA
Founder of the Iroquois
Confederacy

CHIEF JOSEPH
Nez Perce Leader

PETER MACDONALD
Former Chairman of the Navajo
Nation

WILMA MANKILLER
Principal Chief of the Cherokees

OSCEOLO
Seminole Rebel

QUANAH PARKER
Comanche Chief

KING PHILIP
Wampanoag Rebel

POCAHONTAS
Powhatan Peacemaker

PONTIAC
Ottawa Rebel

RED CLOUD
Sioux War Chief

WILL ROGERS
Cherokee Entertainer

SEQUOYAH
Inventor of the Cherokee
Alphabet

SITTING BULL
Chief of the Sioux

TECUMSEH
Shawnee Rebel

JIM THORPE
Sac and Fox Athlete

SARAH WINNEMUCCA
Northern Paiute Writer and
Diplomat

Other titles in preparation

On Indian Leadership

by W. David Baird
Howard A. White Professor of History
Pepperdine University

Authoritative utterance is in thy mouth, perception is in thy heart, and thy tongue is the shrine of justice," the ancient Egyptians said of their king. From him, the Egyptians expected authority, discretion, and just behavior. Homer's *Iliad* suggests that the Greeks demanded somewhat different qualities from their leaders: justice and judgment, wisdom and counsel, shrewdness and cunning, valor and action. It is not surprising that different people living at different times should seek different qualities from the individuals they looked to for guidance. By and large, a people's requirements for leadership are determined by two factors: their culture and the unique circumstances of the time and place in which they live.

Before the late 15th century, when non-Indians first journeyed to what is now North America, most Indian tribes were not ruled by a single person. Instead, there were village chiefs, clan headmen, peace chiefs, war chiefs, and a host of other types of leaders, each with his or her own specific duties. These influential people not only decided political matters but also helped shape their tribe's social, cultural, and religious life. Usually, Indian leaders held their positions because they had won the respect of their peers. Indeed, if a leader's followers at any time decided that he or she was out of step with the will of the people, they felt free to look to someone else for advice and direction.

Thus, the greatest achievers in traditional Indian communities were men and women of extraordinary talent. They were not only skilled at navigating the deadly waters of tribal politics and cultural customs but also able to, directly or indirectly, make a positive and significant difference in the daily life of their followers.

From the beginning of their interaction with Native Americans, non-Indians failed to understand these features of Indian leadership. Early European explorers and settlers merely assumed that Indians had the same relationship with their leaders as non-Indians had with their kings and queens. European monarchs generally inherited their positions and ruled large nations however they chose, often with little regard for the desires or needs of their subjects. As a result, the settlers of Jamestown saw Pocahontas as a "princess" and Pilgrims dubbed Wampanoag leader Metacom "King Philip," envisioning them in roles very different from those in which their own people placed them.

As more and more non-Indians flocked to North America, the nature of Indian leadership gradually began to change. Influential Indians no longer had to take on the often considerable burden of pleasing only their own people; they also had to develop a strategy of dealing with the non-Indian newcomers. In a rapidly changing world, new types of Indian role models with new ideas and talents continually emerged. Some were warriors; others were peacemakers. Some held political positions within their tribes; others were writers, artists, religious prophets, or athletes. Although the demands of Indian leadership altered from generation to generation, several factors that determined which Indian people became prominent in the centuries after first contact remained the same.

Certain personal characteristics distinguished these Indians of achievement. They were intelligent, imaginative, practical, daring, shrewd, uncompromising, ruthless, and logical. They were constant in friendships, unrelenting in hatreds, affectionate with their relatives, and respectful to their God or gods. Of course, no single Native American leader embodied all these qualities, nor these qualities only. But it was these characteristics that allowed them to succeed.

The special skills and talents that certain Indians possessed also brought them to positions of importance. The life of Hiawatha, the legendary founder of the powerful Iroquois Confederacy, displays the value that oratorical ability had for many Indians in power.

The biography of Cochise, the 19th-century Apache chief, illustrates that leadership often required keen diplomatic skills not only in transactions among tribespeople but also in hardheaded negotiations with non-Indians. For others, such as Mohawk Joseph Brant and Navajo Peter MacDonald, a non-Indian education proved advantageous in their dealings with other peoples.

Sudden changes in circumstance were another crucial factor in determining who became influential in Indian communities. King Philip in the 1670s and Geronimo in the 1880s both came to power when their people were searching for someone to lead them into battle against white frontiersmen who had forced upon them a long series of indignities. Seeing the rising discontent of Indians of many tribes in the 1810s, Tecumseh and his brother, the Shawnee prophet Tenskwatawa, proclaimed a message of cultural revitalization that appealed to thousands. Other Indian achievers recognized cooperation with non-Indians as the most advantageous path during their lifetime. Sarah Winnemucca in the late 19th century bridged the gap of understanding between her people and their non-Indian neighbors through the publication of her autobiography *Life Among the Piutes*. Olympian Jim Thorpe in the early 20th century championed the assimilationist policies of the U.S. government and, with his own successes, demonstrated the accomplishments Indians could make in the non-Indian world. And Wilma Mankiller, principal chief of the Cherokees, continues to fight successfully for the rights of her people through the courts and through negotiation with federal officials.

Leadership among Native Americans, just as among all other peoples, can be understood only in the context of culture and history. But the centuries that Indians have had to cope with invasions of foreigners in their homelands have brought unique hardships and obstacles to the Native American individuals who most influenced and inspired others. Despite these challenges, there has never been a lack of Indian men and women equal to these tasks. With such strong leaders, it is no wonder that Native Americans remain such a vital part of this nation's cultural landscape.

1

A DIFFICULT DECISION

Following a snowy trail crisscrossed with animal tracks, 13-year-old Pocahontas moved swiftly through the dark forest. Her footsteps made no sound. Nothing pierced the night's frosty silence but the occasional snap of an icicle in the tree branches high above. Pocahontas, the favorite daughter of a powerful Indian chief, was accustomed to traveling with servants, but on this bitterly cold night in January 1609, she walked alone.

Earlier in the day, Pocahontas's father, Powhatan—*mamanatowick* (great king) of the Powhatan Confederacy in what is now eastern Virginia—had left his home village, Werowocomoco (chief's town), for a temporary encampment in the forest. Accompanying the ruler had been his attendants and several of his wives and children, including Pocahontas. As night fell, Pocahontas had slipped away and headed back to Werowocomoco. She was walking a dangerous path, away from her father and toward his new enemies, the English settlers of the Jamestown colony.

The English colonists had arrived in the region only two years earlier. They had sailed into the "Bay of Chesupiac" (Chesapeake Bay) aboard three British ships—the *Susan Constant*, the *Godspeed*, and the *Discovery*—and anchored on the banks of Powhatan's em-

pire on April 26, 1607. Financed by the Virginia Company, an English investment venture, the small fleet was manned by a collection of hardy, seasoned adventurers. Their mission was to establish an English settlement.

After selecting a site, the colonists began working on their outpost, which they named Jamestown after the English king, James I. Laboring furiously, they erected a fortified trading post, a group of thatched houses, a church, and a storehouse. All their efforts sent a message to the Indians of the region: the English planned to stay.

The Indians resisted the invasion of their land. Many times in the following months they staged small attacks on Jamestown. Powhatan, however, did not want to initiate a full-scale war. He was shrewd enough to realize that these foreigners' weapons—European-made metal hatchets and firearms—were superior to the Indians' arrows.

But as time went by, Powhatan came to suspect that war was unavoidable. The English were growing in number and taking over more land. They displayed no

Traveling aboard three ships—the Susan Constant, *the* Godspeed, *and the* Discovery— *some 100 English colonists arrived on the banks of present-day Virginia on April 26, 1607.*

respect for the native inhabitants of the area and gave no indication that they ever intended to leave.

Powhatan finally abandoned his efforts to keep the peace after a visit from a colonist, Captain John Smith, one morning in January of 1609. The residents of Jamestown had not been able to grow enough food to feed themselves. Many times before, they had requested help from their Indian neighbors, and now Smith arrived in the village of Werowocomoco to ask for aid once again. Powhatan proposed a trade: he would give the colonists 40 baskets of corn if they gave him 40 English swords. Smith refused. The Englishman had no intention of surrendering his precious weapons to potential enemies.

Powhatan then posed the question that had been on his mind continuously since the Englishmen had arrived: When were the colonists going to leave his land? Smith would not give the Indian leader an answer.

A 1590 engraving of an Indian couple sharing a meal of corn, squid, walnuts, and fish. The early English colonists were amazed by the variety of foods available in the Virginia wilderness.

An accomplished storyteller, Captain John Smith assured himself a place in American history through his colorful (though probably largely untrue) tales of his adventures during the early days of Jamestown.

In his memoirs, Smith later maintained that Powhatan was fully aware that the English intended Jamestown to be a permanent colony. Powhatan explained his suspicions that the English had come "hither . . . not for trade, but to invade my people, and possesse my Country." Despite his accusation, Powhatan agreed to negotiate with Smith. He offered the captain about 80 bushels of corn in exchange for a copper kettle.

The deal made, Smith left the meeting with a supply of corn. A few hours later, Powhatan and his family fled Werowocomoco as well, heading for another village, Orapacks, some 50 miles away. Before setting out, Powhatan met with his counselors. Together, they decided that Smith and his men had to be killed.

Pocahontas quickly learned of her father's decree. She may even have been present when he and his counselors made the decision. In any case, Powhatan's order horrified Pocahontas, who had become friendly with the foreigners and had even learned a little of their language. Making her own important decision, she elected to warn them about the terrible danger they faced.

At this point, John Smith and several of his men were still in Werowocomoco. Their boats—a small sailing ship and two barges—had become trapped in the frozen river, and some of Powhatan's tribesmen were assisting the Englishmen by chopping a path through the ice. As soon as the vessels were freed, the colonists planned to return to Jamestown. Waiting for dawn, the unsuspecting Englishmen were gathered around their fire when Pocahontas burst in on them. She told them they were to be killed sometime in the night, then vanished as quickly as she had appeared.

After she had left, Smith and his men loaded their muskets, watched the shadows, and waited. By first light, they saw that the Indians had finished breaking a channel through the ice. Then, led by Smith, the colonists strode to the riverbank, boarded their boats, and sailed with the tide.

It is unclear how or when Pocahontas slipped away from her family and ran back to Werowocomoco to warn the Englishmen of her father's plans. Why she chose to do so is nearly as mysterious. What made Pocahontas willing to defy her father to save these foreigners? Her reasons will never be known for certain, but undoubtedly she had developed an enormous affection for the strangers and their unfamiliar ways. Whatever the girl's motives were as she rushed through the forest, risking her status and possibly even her life, Pocahontas became the first ambassador to mediate between her people and the seafaring English from afar.

2

▿ ▿ ▿

"HIS WILL IS LAWE"

A painting by John White depicting a ceremonial dance held at the Algonkian village of Secotan. In 1586, while living at the English colony of Roanoke in present-day North Carolina, White painted a series of pictures of local Indians. These paintings provide much of the existing information on how the Powhatan Indians lived at the time of Pocahontas's birth.

Pocahontas was born around 1595 in what is now eastern Virginia. She and her people were Algonkians, members of a large, loosely knit family of tribes scattered across northeastern North America. All Algonkian tribes shared the same religion, language, and way of living, but they maintained no regular contact among themselves, trading—or warring—only with those groups closest to them.

Modern archaeologists (scientists who study past human life) believe that Pocahontas's people originally lived in what is now southern Canada. Sometime in the 14th century—about 100 years before Christopher Columbus's 1492 arrival in the New World—the tribe apparently wandered south, eventually settling in the coastal lowlands of present-day Virginia.

Following the area's brackish rivers to the shore, this group of Algonkians, later known as the Powhatans, settled along the Chesapeake Bay in a region now called the Tidewater. The Powhatans soon learned that for food they could rely on the bay, teeming with mussels and oysters, and on the woodlands, which supported large numbers of deer, squirrels, raccoons, rabbits, opossums, and beavers. In the rich soil along the riverbanks, the Indians planted corn, beans, and squash. During the summer, they gathered berries, and in the fall, hickory nuts, walnuts, and chestnuts. In this land of plenty, the Algonkian people thrived.

The Powhatans revered nature in all its forms—water, sky, and earth. Among their deities were the gentle god Ahone, nature spirits called *manitous*, and a host of minor spirits, including the kindly *quiyoughcosuck* and the vicious *tagkanysough*.

The Powhatans' most powerful deity was Okewas, a vengeful and fearsome god who had created the order of the world and who oversaw its moral code. Individuals

The Indians of Virginia relied on the ocean for much of their food. On fishing trips, such as this one painted by White, they used spears and nets to kill fish or caught them in traps known as weirs (far left). The fire in the dugout canoe was probably set to provide light, suggesting that White's illustration represents a nighttime expedition.

who violated that code were likely to have accidents or runs of bad luck—punishments from Okewas. To atone for their misdeeds, transgressors offered shell beads or tobacco to Okewas, whose image was present in every village temple and always carried into battle.

Mediating between gods and humans were priests, called—like the deities—quiyoughcosucks. These individuals performed ceremonies in the village temple, cured illnesses with herbs, prayed for favorable weather conditions for the crops, predicted the future, and gave advice to the village leader, or *werowance*.

A werowance—or, in the case of a female leader, *weronsqua*—inherited his or her position through election or inheritance. Endowed with supreme governmental and religious power over their tribe, these leaders received deep respect and total obedience from their people. They had the power to order punishments—including death—for lawbreakers, and their orders could not be questioned.

Werowances lived in greater luxury than their subjects, wearing more elegant clothing, dwelling in finer houses, and eating better food. Even in death, they had special privileges. When an ordinary person died, his family wrapped his body in a grass mat and buried it. But when a werowance died, tribe members carefully removed and cleaned his skeleton, sewed it back into his preserved skin, and took it to the village temple. There, they placed it on a platform with the preserved bodies of earlier werowances, all of them guarded by an image of Okewas.

It was into this elite werowance class that Pocahontas's father Powhatan—originally named Wahunsonacock—was born, probably in the 1540s. His birthplace, the Algonkian village of Powhatan, lay on the James River, just south of present-day Richmond, Virginia. When he reached maturity, Wahunsonacock inherited both the leadership of the village and its name. At the same time, he assumed hereditary rulership over seven other river-

A quiyoughcosuck, or tribal priest. Quiyoughcosucks presided over ceremonies and cared for the ill. They were also thought to have the ability to predict the future.

side tribes, bringing the population of his confederacy to about 1,750. After claiming his birthright, Powhatan moved to expand his holdings, eventually conquering most of the neighboring tribes. By the early 17th century, he ruled about 7,500 people from some 30 tribes.

Powhatan had been unhappily aware of Europeans and their interest in his empire for most of his life. In about 1560, when he was still a teenager, a small Spanish expedition had sailed into Chesapeake Bay, landed, and made contact with the Powhatans of the region. For

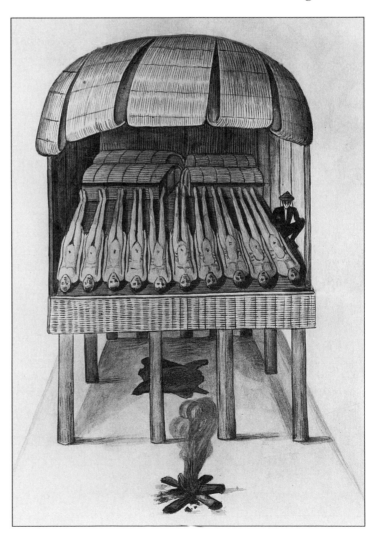

When a werowance (village leader) died, the Powhatans placed his preserved corpse on a raised platform inside the village temple. Along the temple's right wall in this John White painting appears a carved image of Okewas, the Indians' most powerful deity. The deerskin under the platform possibly marked the spot where a quiyoughcosuck might come to pray.

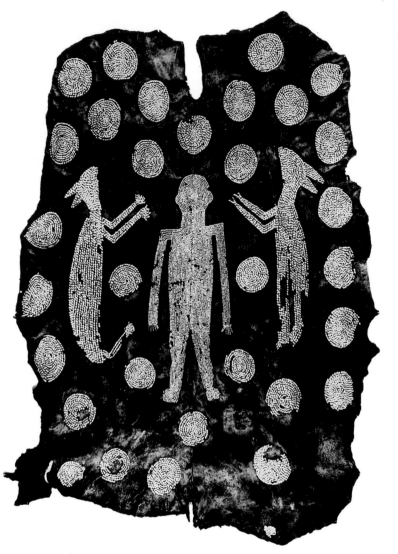

This buckskin robe, decorated with shell beads, was made by Virginia Indians in about 1600. Today, it is known as "Powhatan's mantle," although there is no evidence that it ever belonged to the Indian leader.

reasons historians have never understood, a brother of a local Indian leader—quite possibly, someone known to the young Powhatan—decided to join the Spaniards. They took him to their settlement in present-day Cuba, baptized him, and gave him the name Don Luis Velasco.

The Indian Don Luis visited Spain, met the Spanish king Philip II, and eventually agreed to recross the ocean and guide a party of Spanish missionary priests into his home territory. The Spanish and the Indians got along peacefully for several months, but then Don Luis apparently underwent a change of heart. Suddenly determined to renounce the Europeans and rejoin his own people, he led a war party into the priests' settlement. The Indians killed all the foreigners but one, a boy who later recounted the story. A year after the massacre, in 1571, Spanish troops sailed into Chesapeake Bay and killed 30 Powhatan Indians.

The next major confrontation between the Powhatan people and Europeans came in 1597, when three English ships arrived at Roanoke Island, off the coast of present-day North Carolina, and built a settlement. Three years later, English supply ships found the settlement completely destroyed and its inhabitants missing. The exact fate of the lost colony of Roanoke still remains a mystery. Later English settlers, however, did hear rumors that Roanoke Island's luckless residents had been slaughtered by Powhatan tribesmen.

When Don Luis arrived from Spain with the missionaries, Powhatan was about 25 years old. Whether or not he took part in the massacre of the priests or witnessed the subsequent Spanish slaughter of the Indians is not known, but he must have been aware of the events. And whatever happened on Roanoke Island would have made news among the coastal tribes and been reported from one group to another.

In any case, from that point on, Europeans appeared on the Chesapeake's shores with increasing frequency, and Powhatan's anxiety grew. He was not sure what these white men wanted, but he was certain that their arrival could mean nothing but trouble for his people.

Between the years of Don Luis's return in 1570 and the arrival of the *Susan Constant*, the *Discovery*, and the *Godspeed* in 1607, Powhatan showed himself to be a

forceful, even autocratic leader. To protect his people from the threat of European conquest, he assembled a strong military force. He also made himself a very wealthy man, collecting tribute from his subjects and filling his royal warehouse to overflowing with corn, venison, precious shells, pearls, and furs.

In his 1612 book *The Historie of Travaile into Virginia Britannia,* English colonist William Strachey wrote about Powhatan, his supreme powers, and his complex political system. Like the old European feudal barons, Strachey observed, Powhatan supplied his minor chiefs with military defense in exchange for their allegiance and tribute. Strachey also noted that Powhatan's role as a maker and enforcer of law was similar to those of the European monarchs who ruled by "divine right": "When he pleaseth his will is lawe, and must be obeyed, not only as a king, but half as a god, his People esteeme him so," noted Strachey of the Native American ruler.

Powhatan is known to have had many wives and possibly as many as 20 sons and 10 daughters. According to historical sources, his daughter Matoaka was his favorite. As a baby, her cheerful, outgoing nature touched everyone, including her powerful father. Fittingly, her name meant "playful" or "frolicsome." But Matoaka was the child's clan name, to be used only within her family. To preserve the name's magical powers of protection, her people also gave her a public name: Pocahontas, which meant "mischievous" or "frisky." Little is known about Pocahontas's very early years, but the fact that she inspired these names suggests that she was unusually lighthearted and winsome.

Despite the sporadic appearance of European ships on the Tidewater coast, Pocahontas's early childhood seems to have been peaceful and happy. Historians have found no record of her mother. Like most children of the

During Powhatan's reign, his people lived in large villages similar to the one that appears in this engraving by Theodor de Bry based on a John White painting. Lining a central pathway are fields of corn, tobacco, pumpkins, and sunflowers. In the top right of the engraving, marked by the letter F, is a special structure in which a villager could sit and guard the fields against birds and other animals.

werowance class, she was probably taken away from her mother at birth and raised in her father's household. As a member of the royal family, she would not have been expected to do the usual labor that fell to Powhatan girls and women. Gardening, hauling water, collecting wood, preparing food, and sewing deerskins were not jobs required of Powhatan's favorite daughter. Instead, Pocahontas probably spent her days swimming in the

White's portrait of the wife and daughter of a werowance. The woman's right arm rests in a decorative sling adorned with pearls and copper. The copper and the doll held by her daughter were probably obtained from the English. Pocahontas was only a few years older than the girl shown here when the first English settlers arrived in Virginia.

Tidewater rivers and racing along the narrow forest paths trodden down by animals and followed by hunters.

As carefree as her childhood was, Pocahontas seems to have had a quieter, more contemplative side. At an early age, she sat next to her all-powerful father during meetings and ceremonies. A poised demeanor was undoubtedly demanded of her during these solemn occasions.

Her friend Captain John Smith recorded still another aspect of young Pocahontas's personality. In his book *Generall Historie of Virginia* (1624), written seven years after her death, he remembered Pocahontas, even as a girl, as having a "compassionate pitifull [sympathetic] heart" that "gave me much cause to respect her." Throughout his life, Smith acknowledged that the royal child's extraordinary kindness had earned not only his admiration but also his undying gratitude. Without Pocahontas and her sympathy, Smith knew he and his fellow colonists would never have survived in the wilds of their adopted Virginia home.

A 16th-century drawing of the English fleet battling the Spanish armada in 1588. The armada's defeat marked the end of Spain's reign as Europe's dominant sea power. Thereafter, English ships carrying colonists to the New World could freely sail the Atlantic.

3

ENGLAND EXPANDS

In 1566, about the time that Powhatan was consolidating his empire in North America, another monarch— Mary, Queen of Scots—gave birth to a son in far-off Scotland. The boy, who became James VI of Scotland at the age of one, would eventually become James I of England, a powerful sovereign whose reign would strongly affect the "great king" across the Atlantic Ocean.

When James was 21 years old, his mother died on the headsman's block, executed by her cousin Queen Elizabeth I of England for trying to assume the English crown. In 1603, when Elizabeth died, James succeeded to the English throne, remaining king for the next 22 years.

During most of Elizabeth's reign, the Catholic countries of Portugal, Spain, and France posed a major threat to Protestant England's security. Furthermore, these nations, Spain in particular, had acquired a near monopoly on trading with—and robbing—the inhabitants of the New World. Laden with gold, silver, and jewels, Spanish treasure ships sailed home from the Americas in a steady stream. Elizabeth, imperious, proud, and totally dedicated to England, looked with displeasure on the Spanish gains.

Meanwhile, British shipbuilders had been turning out an array of extraordinarily seaworthy and, for their time, speedy sailing vessels. Commanding these magnificent ships, Sir Francis Drake, Sir John Hawkins, and other daring Elizabethan captains began to harass the Spanish, bearing down on their treasure ships and seizing the riches stolen from the Indians of the Americas.

Sparked by sharp religious and political quarrels, and increased by British high seas piracy, Spain's antagonism toward England intensified steadily. Finally, King Philip of Spain decided to conquer his northern enemy, get rid of Elizabeth, and seize the English crown for himself. In the summer of 1588, he mounted the greatest invasion fleet the world had ever known—130 ships, 8,350 sailors, 2,080 galley slaves, and 19,290 soldiers—and set it on course for England. Philip had absolute faith in his seemingly invincible armada.

But by then, the British had become true masters of the sea. After pounding the Spanish forces for nine days, the English navy—led by Sir Francis Drake and aided by a providential southwest wind—sent the mighty armada scurrying homeward. The battle, which involved an immense loss of ships and lives, dealt Spanish confidence a devastating blow and marked the beginning of that nation's decline as a colonial power.

The defeat of the Spanish armada also at last gave England the opportunity to travel safely across the Atlantic and establish its own colonies in the Americas. The English had an array of motives for colonization. First, their own country was becoming overpopulated. "The land grows weary of its people," observed one writer of the time. The Americas appeared to be an excellent place to export the poor and unemployed of England. Second, English merchants wanted new markets for their goods, particularly woolens. They hoped to persuade the Indians to swap furs for woven blankets and coats. Third, the English desired gold, and they believed there was plenty of it in the New World.

During the reign of James I (1603–25), England began in earnest its colonization of North America.

Still another driving force behind colonization was exploration. Europeans, who had an insatiable appetite for the spices and silks of India and the Far East, had long dreamed of finding a short route to these lands. Many expected to find such a passage up one of the rivers and bays that dotted the American coastline. Finally, the Protestant British believed it was their duty to convert as many Indians as possible to their faith. The Roman Catholic Spanish had already made formidable inroads in converting the native populations of South and Central America, and the English wanted to reach the North American Indians' souls before the hated Spaniards could get to them.

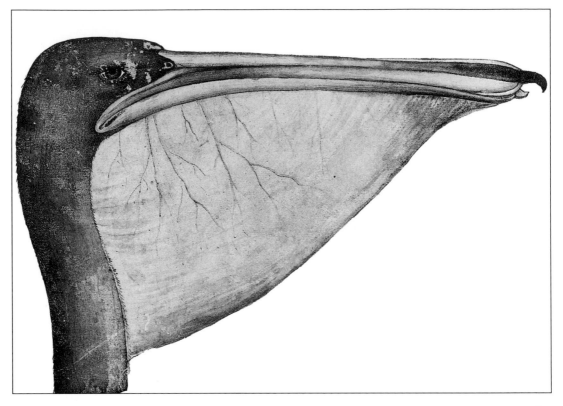

By 1600, England had already made several failed attempts to establish outposts in North America. However, British colonial expansion did not begin in earnest until James was crowned king. King James enthusiastically supported the founding of colonies in various parts of the globe, including Massachusetts, Bermuda, Newfoundland, and India.

The colonization of Virginia, though, was of particular interest to him. James had a keen curiosity for the plants and animals native to areas the English considered exotic. The flora and fauna of coastal Virginia especially fascinated him. Several years after the founding of Jamestown, James counted among his royal treasures a pair of flying squirrels that had been captured in the Virginia forest.

A John White illustration of a brown pelican, a bird native to the Tidewater region. King James was fascinated by exotic flora and fauna. His hobby spurred his desire to establish an English colony in Virginia.

On April 10, 1605, James I stamped the Great Seal of England on the first Virginia charter. This charter called for the formation of two colonies: North Virginia, in what is now New England, and South Virginia, in what is now the Tidewater area of the present-day state of Virginia.

The two groups of colonists recruited to establish these settlements differed greatly in background and outlook. The North Virginia settlers were Puritans, members of a religious sect that sought to reform the Protestant church. James had proven hostile to their beliefs, so many Puritans elected to emigrate to North America in search of religious freedom. For the most part, the Puritans were solemn, hardworking people. They looked down on their South Virginia counterparts, whom they considered too lazy to succeed either at building a colony or converting the native population. In the late 17th century, Boston clergyman Cotton Mather expressed the opinions of his

A portion of the list of the first Jamestown colonists, compiled by Captain John Smith and reproduced in his 1624 book Generall Historie of Virginia. *The large number of gentlemen (designated by "Gent.") in the group impeded the early growth of the colony. Men of this social class were unaccustomed to performing manual labor and farming the land, tasks crucial to their survival in the Virginia wilderness.*

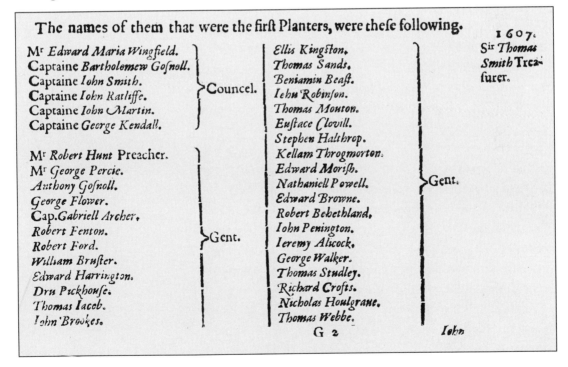

The names of them that were the first Planters, were these following.

1607.

Councel.
Mr *Edward Maria Wingfield.*
Captaine *Bartholemew Gosnoll.*
Captaine *Iohn Smith.*
Captaine *Iohn Ratliffe.*
Captaine *Iohn Martin.*
Captaine *George Kendall.*

Gent.

Mr *Robert Hunt* Preacher.
Mr *George Percie.*
Anthony Gosnoll.
George Flower.
Cap.*Gabriell Archer.*
Robert Fenton.
Robert Ford.
William Bruster.
Edward Harrington.
Dru Pickhouse.
Thomas Iacob.
Iohn Brookes.

Ellis Kingston.
Thomas Sands.
Beniamin Beast.
Iehu Robinson.
Thomas Mouton.
Eustace Clovill.
Stephen Halthrop.
Kellam Throgmorton.
Edward Morish.
Nathaniell Powell.
Edward Browne.
Robert Behethland.
Iohn Penington.
Ieremy Alicock.
George Walker.
Thomas Studley.
Richard Crofts.
Nicholas Houlgrave.
Thomas Webbe.

Gent.

Sir *Thomas Smith* Treasurer.

G 2

Iohn

ancestors by writing that the settlers of South Virginia were "the Refuse of the English Nation." Mather's sentiments were, in fact, largely true. Most of the men who had settled Jamestown were unemployed, disinherited, and landless. Many were signed up for the journey by their families, who considered them men of little promise or, in some cases, even embarrassments to the family name.

Despite their dubious past, the South Virginia recruits included many men who would play crucial roles in the early history of colonial America. One such colonist was George Percy. Percy's older brother, the earl of Northumberland, was imprisoned in the Tower of London for allegedly participating in a plot to kill King James. With his reputation irredeemably soiled by his brother's notoriety, Percy was pleased to have the chance to start a new life in Virginia. Throughout his stay in Jamestown, Percy kept a well-written account of his experiences. His writings are one of the most valuable sources of information about the founding of the colony.

Another renowned Jamestown colonist was Christopher Newport, commander of the *Susan Constant*. Long before setting off for Virginia, Newport had gained a reputation as an able seaman. In 1588, he had joined Sir Francis Drake in battle with the Spanish armada, and in 1592, he made his fortune by capturing the *Madre de Dios*, the jewel of the Spanish treasure fleet. Newport had not signed on to be a permanent resident at Jamestown. He was hired by the Virginia Company only to transport colonists and supplies between England and North America. In between his transatlantic voyages, Newport was to explore the inland rivers near the settlement.

In addition to his skill as a captain, Newport was known as a strict disciplinarian, an asset the Virginia Company recognized as essential to managing the unruly crew it

George Percy produced an informative chronicle of the early days of Jamestown. He would later serve as the colony's governor.

had assembled. The stern captain's ability to control his men was tested soon after the *Susan Constant* set sail for Virginia on December 20, 1606. The crew member who presented the greatest challenge to Newport's attempts to keep order was John Smith, who would become the most famous of all the Jamestown settlers.

At the age of 29, Smith had already seen enough excitement for a lifetime. Enlisting in the army when he was little more than a teenager, he had spent four years fighting for the British crown, then joined the Austrian army to battle the Turks in Transylvania. He had been captured and given as a present to a Turkish ruler, but

he escaped to Russia, where he was once again enslaved. After killing his master, he had fought his way across Russia and returned to England in 1604, only two years before he was on the high seas headed for Virginia.

Smith's adventures provided him with countless stories to amuse his fellow crewmen during their four-month trip. But on the way, his bravado also got him into trouble. After being charged with attempting to incite a mutiny aboard the *Susan Constant*, Smith was placed under arrest by Captain Newport and locked in chains for the remainder of the voyage.

On the morning of April 26, 1607, the *Susan Constant*, followed by the *Godspeed* and the *Discovery*, finally set its anchor down six miles off the shore of Chesapeake Bay. The crew's shouts of excitement echoed over the

A 19th-century rendering of the landing of the Jamestown colonists on the shore of Virginia.

deck. The 18 stormy weeks at sea had taken the lives of 16 of the original 120 crewmen, and all the survivors were ecstatic to see land again.

Smith was still chained in the depths of the ship when it anchored. Hearing the cries of the crew, he managed to escape just long enough to catch a glimpse of the shoreline. Looking at the New World for the first time, Smith must have wondered what the future would hold for him in this strange and awesome land. But despite his excitement, Smith, now a prisoner of his own people, had no way of guessing that he was about to embark on the greatest adventure of his life.

An 1845 watercolor of the site of Jamestown near the confluence of the James and Chickahominy rivers. The ruins to the left were a portion of a building from the original settlement.

4

GUNS AND ARROWS

As soon as the three English ships anchored, an exploratory party was formed. Its members were to undertake an initial investigation of the land that was to be their new home.

Fearing an Indian attack, the party left the ships under the cover of night. Despite their caution, the Englishmen were soon spotted. According to George Percy,

> There came the Savages creeping upon all foure, from the Hills, like Beares; with their Bowes in their mouthes [they] charged us . . . [and] hurt Captaine Gabriell Archer in both his hands, and a [sailor] in two place of the body.

Captain Newport fired his musket at the attackers. Never having heard gunfire, the Indians were terrified. Percy wrote that "they retired into the Woods with a great noise."

Somewhat shaken, the explorers returned to their ships. There they turned their attention to the three boxes that had been given to them by James I with the instruction that they not be disturbed until the men had reached Virginia. The colonists at last opened the boxes to find a list of goals that the king expected them to accomplish. The settlers' first mission was to try to discover a water route to the Orient. They were also to look for deposits of gold and silver to ensure that the financial backers of the colony received a good return on their investment.

Finally, they were to search for the settlers of the lost colony of Roanoke.

The three boxes also contained instructions for the formation of a council that would be the ruling body of the new colony. The list of council men included the captains of the three ships and Edward Maria Wingfield, who was designated as the colony's president as well. Choosing Wingfield to be the president was shrewd. He was from a distinguished family and had a military background that the king knew would serve the colony well if the settlers had to battle Indians.

One name that appeared on the list of councilmen surprised everyone. John Smith, who was still in chains because of his alleged attempted mutiny, was to be part of this august body. Wingfield and the other newly designated members of the council were hesitant to accept the king's confidence in Smith. They voted to delay Smith's initiation into the council until they arrived at a verdict regarding his mutiny charge.

Before transacting any business, the councilmen took an oath of allegiance to the Protestant King James. James wanted to make sure that they were all not only loyal subjects but also devout Protestants. Otherwise, he feared that Catholicism might blossom among the English settlers living so far from their homeland.

The council's first official order of business was to choose a site for the new colony. President Wingfield and the other councilmen embarked on a series of exploratory missions along a waterway they named the James River. Traveling westward in a lightweight open boat known as a shallop, they determined (incorrectly) that the river might provide passage to the Pacific Ocean. They continued on, confident in the belief that they had already satisfied the first of James's three goals for their enterprise.

POWHATAN'S REALM IN THE EARLY 17TH CENTURY

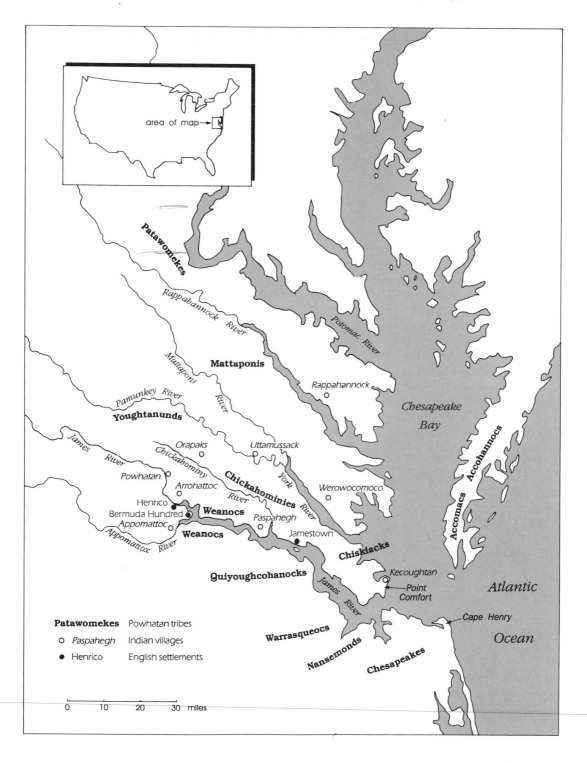

area of map →

Patawomekes

Rappahannock River

Potomac River

Mattaponis

Mattaponi River

Pamunkey River

Rappahannock ○

Chesapeake Bay

Youghtanunds

James River

Orapaks ○

Chickahominy

Uttamussack

Chickahominies

York River

Powhatan ○

Arrohattoc ○

Werowocomoco ○

Henrico ●

Bermuda Hundred ●

Weanocs

Appomattoc ○

Paspahegh ○

Appomattox River

Weanocs

Jamestown ●

Chiskiacks

Accomacs

Accohannocs

Guiyoughcohanocks

James River

Kecoughtan ○
Point Comfort

Atlantic Ocean

Cape Henry

Warrasqueocs

Nansemonds

Chesapeakes

Patawomekes   Powhatan tribes

○ *Paspahegh*   Indian villages

● Henrico   English settlements

0   10   20   30   miles

George Percy was struck by the beauty of the river. He wrote that

> many branches . . . runne flowing through the Woods with great plentie of fish of all kindes . . . and all the grounds [along the river are] bespread with many sweet and delicate flowres of divers colours and kindes . . . as though [they were] in any Garden or Orchard in England.

Close to the point where the James and Chickahominy rivers meet, the colonists discovered a site they considered ideal for their settlement. There they found a peninsula that seemed convenient yet isolated enough that they doubted any Spanish ships could surprise them with a raid. About two miles long and one mile wide, the peninsula also had about 1,550 acres of rich soil for growing crops.

However, the English did not consider the site's native inhabitants. Because it was so conveniently situated, the James River had once been a route into a favorite hunting ground of the Paspahegh Indians. They had abandoned the area, though, because of its vulnerability to hurricanes. With no Indians in sight, the English assumed they had found a secluded, defensible location. Unbeknownst to them, the peninsula was actually in the middle of Chief Powhatan's empire.

At the end of April, Captain Newport and a small crew set off to explore more of the region. When they stopped at the place where the James River flows into the Chesapeake Bay, which they named Point Comfort, the colonists were seen by four Indians on the shore. The men rowed the boat toward them. Newport placed his right hand over his heart, a gesture he hoped would convey that he and his crew came in peace. The Indians understood and laid down their bows and arrows. They then invited the Englishmen to their village, Kecoughtan, which was located a few miles north of Point Comfort.

There the colonists met Pochins, Pocahontas's half brother and the werowance of Kecoughtan. The English and the Indians sat down to a feast. Afterward, the colonists were treated to a ceremonial dance and shared a peace pipe with their hosts.

For a time, the goodwill between the Indians and the newcomers continued. Whenever the English sailed up the James River, Indians along the shore shouted out to welcome them. On May 4, the werowance of Paspahegh, a village about 10 miles northwest of Jamestown, followed Pochins's example and entertained a group of the foreigners.

Several weeks later, the werowance of Paspahegh, along with 100 warriors, came to visit Jamestown. They carried with them the carcass of a large deer, which they probably were intending to present as a gift to the colonists. After the Indians and the English exchanged greetings, the werowance asked the settlers to lay down their arms. Afraid the visit might be a ploy of the Indians to catch them off guard, the English refused. The werowance and his men were clearly offended.

Tensions grew even greater when the colonists saw a warrior running off with an English hatchet. Percy recorded that the owner

> tooke it from [the Indian] by force, and also strooke him over the arme. Presently another Savage seeing that, came fiercely at our man with a wooden sword, thinking to beat out his braines. The werowance of Paspahegh saw us take to our arms, and went suddenly away with all his company in great anger.

Eight days later, the Paspahegh Indians attacked Jamestown. Any chance for the Indians and the colonists to coexist peacefully was gone.

During the tense months that followed, the colonists' contempt for the Indians was almost universal. All

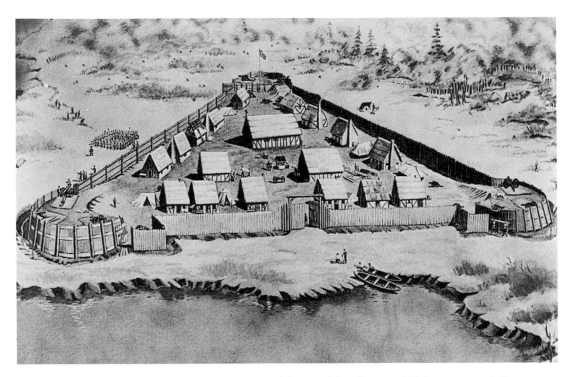

Indians, in the settlers' eyes, were savages who could only be redeemed if they adopted Protestantism. The Indians' views about the invaders in their territory, however, varied considerably. Some Indians were still interested in trading with the Englishmen. They tended to be friendly, though cautious, in their dealings with the colonists. Other Indians resented the intruders. Their reaction to the Englishmen's presence was to stage sporadic attacks on the fort or on colonists wandering through the forest on hunting or exploring expeditions.

The residents of Jamestown were baffled by the differing behavior of the many groups of Indians under Powhatan's sway. In the Europeans' experience, a people united under one ruler obeyed that leader completely. They did not understand that the tribes within Powhatan's empire felt fairly free to think and act as they wished.

A 20th-century artist's conception of the fort constructed at Jamestown within a month of the colonists' arrival. The high, triangular palisade reveals the extent to which the colonists feared Indian attacks.

The colonists also had trouble adapting their methods of battle to encounters in the Virginia wilderness. Fearing Indian attacks, they took to wearing the metal armor they had brought with them from England whenever they left the fort. Although the bulky armor helped protect them from their enemies' arrows, it was stiflingly hot, making hiking through the forest under the scorching summer sun nearly unbearable.

The colonists also wore armor whenever a band of Indians approached the fort and sent a barrage of arrows over its walls. But by the time the Englishmen had donned their heavy breastplates and helmets, hoisted their muskets onto props, poured powder into their guns, and fired off a round of bullets, the Indians were usually long gone.

Out in the Virginia woods, the colonists had little more success in fighting off Indian attackers. There they tried to defend themselves with poleaxes and swords, but their enemies rarely obliged them by standing still long enough to be struck down by these weapons.

The only Indian the colonists seemed to trust completely was young Pocahontas. Some historical documents show that, accompanied by her attendants, she courageously ventured into Jamestown several times between May and December of 1607, despite the hostility that the colonists felt toward her people.

Possibly during this time she first got to know Captain John Smith. With his flamboyant past, he seemed an unlikely choice of a friend for the Indian girl. Perhaps they were bound together by a mutual curiosity about each other's language. A practical man, Smith knew that if he had knowledge of the Powhatan language he stood a better chance of surviving in the Indians' land. Under Pocahontas's tutelage, Smith learned to translate some English sentences into Powhatan. Years later, he added a brief dictionary of Powhatan words to his *Generall Historie*. To illustrate Powhatan sentence structure, he included the following example: "Kekaten Pokahontas Patiaquagh niugh tanks Manotyens neer mowchick rawrenock Audough," which Smith translated as, "Bid Pokahuntas bring hither two little baskets, and I will give her white beads to make her a chaine."

A John White watercolor of a werowance wearing ceremonial clothing and body paint and carrying a bow and quiver. Although the gun-toting colonists had superior weapons, the Powhatans' skill as warriors gave them a greater advantage in battle.

In return for his lessons, Smith taught Pocahontas about the colonists' language and customs. Perhaps even more instructive was the girl's firsthand chance to watch the young colony grow. During the months that Pocahontas visited Jamestown, she became familiar with English ways as she watched the colonists construct homes and clear land for fields.

She probably also saw the colonists build a makeshift church by nailing one of the ship's sails to three or four trees. Church services were held there twice a day, in the morning and in the evening. Under the guidance of the chaplain, Reverend Robert Hunt, the settlers read from the Bible and the Book of Common Prayer. They also recited a special prayer for Jamestown, for themselves, and for the "heathen" Indians:

> Almighty God . . . we therefore beseech thee to bless us and this plantation which we and our nation have begun in thy fear and for thy glory . . . even here where Satan's throne is, Lord let our labour be blessed in labouring for the conversion of the heathen.

By midsummer, the colonists' prayers grew more desperate. Their food supply had diminished drastically, and they were too afraid of meeting up with angry Indians to leave the fort to hunt or fish. The situation grew so dire that Captain Newport set sail for England on June 22. He promised to return in about five months with more supplies and colonists.

During those dark days, George Percy's diary entries no longer praised the beauty of the colonists' surroundings. Instead, he dwelt on their tremendous suffering:

> [Our] food was but a small can of Barlie sod in water to five men a day, our drinke cold water taken out of the River, which was at flood verie Salt, at a low tide full of slime and filth, which was the destruction of many of our men.

By the end of the summer, half the colonists were dead.

Because many doe desire to know the manner of their Language, I haue inserted these few words.

KA katorawincs yowo. What call you this.
Nemarough, a man.
Crenepo, a woman.
Marowancheſſo, a boy.
Yehawkans, Houſes.
Matchcores, Skins, or garments.
Mockaſins, Shooes.
Tuſſan, Beds. Pokatawer, Fire.
Attawp, A bow. Attonce, Arrowes.
Monacookes, Swords.
Aumouhhowgh, A Target.
Pawcuſſacks, Gunnes.
Tomahacks, Axes.
Tockahacks, Pickaxes.
Pameſacks, Kniues.
Accowprets, Sheares.
Pawpecones, Pipes. Mattaſſin, Copper
Vſſawaſſin, Iron, Braſſe, Silver, or any white mettall. Muſſes, Woods.
Attaſkuſſ, Leaues, weeds, or graſſe.
Chepſin, Land. Shacquohocan. A ſtone.
Wepenter, A cookold.
Suckahanna, Water. Noughmaſſ, Fiſh.
Copotone, Sturgeon.
Weghſhaughes, Fleſh.
Sawwehone, Bloud.
Netoppew, Friends.
Marrapough, Enemies.
Maskapow, the worſt of the enemies.
Mawchick chammay, The beſt of friends
Caſacunnakack, peya quagh acquintan vttaſantaſough, In how many daies will there come hither any more Engliſh Ships.

Their Numbers.

Necut, 1. Ningh, 2. Nuſſ, 3. Yowgh, 4.
Paranske, 5. Comotinch, 6. Toppawoſſ, 7
Nuſſwaſh, 8. Kekatawgh, 9. Kaskeke 10
They count no more but by tennes as followeth.
Caſe, how many.
Ninghſapooeksku, 20.
Nuſſapooeksku, 30.

Yowghapooeksku, 40.
Parankeſtaſſapooekſku, 50.
Comatinchtaſſapoockſku, 60.
Nuſſwaſhtaſſapooekſku, 70.
Kekataughtaſſapooekſku, 90.
Necuttoughtyſinough, 100.
Necuttweunquaough, 1000.
Rawcoſowghs, Dayes.
Keſkowghes, Sunnes.
Toppquough. Nights.
Nepawweſhowghs, Moones.
Pawpaxſoughes, Yeares.
Pummahumps, Starres.
Oſies, Heavens.
Okees, Gods.
Quiyoughcoſoughs, Pettie Gods, and their affinities.
Righcomoughes, Deaths.
Kekughes, Liues.
Mowchick woyawgh tawgh noeragh kaquere mecher, I am very hungry? what ſhall I eate?
Tawnor nehiegh Powhatan, Where dwels Powhatan.
Mache, nehiegh yourewgh, Orapaks. Now he dwels a great way hence at Orapaks.
Vittapitchewayne anpechitchs nehawper Werowacomoco, You lie, he ſtaid ever at Werowacomoco.
Kator nehiegh mattagh neer vtt-pitchewayne, Truely he is there I doe not lie.
Spaughtynere keragh werowance mawmarinough kekate wawgh peyaquaugh. Run you then to the King Maymarynough and bid him come hither.
Vtteke, e peya weyack wighwhip, Get you gone, & come againe quickly.
Kekaten Pokahontas patiaquagh niugh tanks manotyens neer mowchick rawrenock audowgh, Bid Pokahontas bring hither two little Baskets, and I will giue her white Beads to make her a Chaine.   F I N I S.

Soon after arriving in Virginia, John Smith set about learning the Powhatans' language, aided by his tutor, Pocahontas. This brief dictionary appeared in his Generall Historie.

The survivors might have been doomed as well if it were not for the aid provided to them by young Pocahontas. At her instigation, a group of Powhatan men arrived at the fort in September with a supply of half-ripe corn. She also told John Smith of certain tribes that were eager to trade food to the colonists. Smith followed her suggestions and found her half brother Pochins particularly receptive. His people gave the dying Englishmen corn and fish. Another nearby tribe, the Quiyoughcohanocks, provided Smith with wild game.

Blustery and boastful, John Smith was not a modest man. But he was forever candid about how much he and the other colonists relied on the help of one young girl as they struggled to survive the early days of Jamestown. Smith later held that Pocahontas was "the instrument [that saved] this colony from death, famine and utter confusion."

The captain also insisted that if, lacking her aid, the infant colony had been allowed to flounder and eventually dissolve, "Virginia might have [lain] as it was at our first arrival." In the days to come, many of Pocahontas's people would look back fondly on that very time before Powhatan's empire had ever been seen or coveted by the white invaders.

POWHATAN

Held this state & fashion when Capt. Smith
was deliuered to him prifoner
1607

5

POWHATAN'S AMBASSADOR

This illustration, which appeared on a 1612 map of Smith's explorations, depicts Chief Powhatan during his first meeting with the captain. Decades later, Smith recalled: "Their Emperor proudly [lay] upon a bedstead a foot high, upon ten or twelve mats, richly hung with many chains of great pearls around his neck. . . . [His] grave and majestic countenance . . . drove me into admiration."

With Pocahontas's help and a store of food, the colonists' confidence that they would survive through the winter of 1607 was restored. Smith, however, knew the food would not last long. He wanted to obtain as many provisions as possible before his new trading partners changed their minds about dealing with the white men.

On one trading expedition, Smith, accompanied by two other colonists and two Indian guides, traveled far up the Chickahominy River. About 30 miles from Jamestown, the river became so narrow that even the crew's small canoe could not continue on. Disembarking, the travelers set about making lunch while they planned their next move. Smith announced that he wanted to explore the area while the others prepared the meal. Taking one of the guides with him, he headed into the forest.

Within minutes, Smith was surprised by a whizzing sound. Before he could figure out what was happening, he realized an arrow had pierced his thigh. Looking up, he saw two Indians with their bowstrings pulled taut, ready to shoot more arrows at him. Smith reached for his gun and fired back. Neither his bullets nor his assailants' arrows reached their marks.

As Smith reloaded his musket, he realized his Indian enemies were not alone. Almost 200 others emerged from

51

the brush and descended upon him. In a panic, his guide cried out that Smith was a white werowance. His words probably saved the captain's life. The attackers were afraid to kill a man with so much power, so they took their captive alive and brought him to their leader, Powhatan's brother Opechancanough.

With his modest command of the Indian's language, Smith was hesitant to even try appealing to the mighty Opechancanough for his freedom. Instead, he pulled a compass out of his pocket and handed it to the werowance. Opechancanough had never seen such an object. He was intrigued by the compass, but also a little frightened by it. Fearing it might be a charm that the Englishman could use to cause him harm, Opechancanough decided to take Smith to his brother and let the all-powerful Powhatan decide the fate of the prisoner.

Escorted by a crowd of guards, Smith marched to Werowocomoco. The first white man ever to enter the village, he must have been in awe of the thriving, prosperous settlement. The starving colonists were spend-

This narrative engraving from Generall Historie *illustrates Smith's tale of his abduction by Pamunkey warriors after a brief skirmish in a Tidewater swamp.*

How they tooke him prisoner in the Oaze 1607.

C. Smith bindeth a saluage to his arme fighteth with the King of Pamaunkee and all his company, and slew 3 of them.

ing the freezing winter shivering in makeshift shelters. In comparison, Powhatan's people seemed to be living in luxury. The village included more than 100 houses flanked by 200 cultivated acres. Smith could see that in a matter of months the Powhatans' well-tended gardens would provide a wealth of corn, beans, and pumpkins for their growing population.

Perhaps most impressive of all was the great Powhatan's residence. The dwelling, called a longhouse, was constructed of a wooden framework covered with reed mats and lined with strips of bark. Resting behind a stockade formed by rows of poles nearly 12 feet high, the magnificent house stretched some 60 feet in length.

As Smith was led through its entrance, his eyes were met by those of "more than two hundred . . . grim Courtiers." Then he spied Powhatan himself, seated beside a roaring fire as he gazed impassively at the helpless Englishman. Recalling the event decades later, Smith's impressions remained vivid. "Such a Majestie as I cannot expresse," Smith wrote of the chief in his *Generall Historie*, "nor yet have often seene in Pagan or Christian."

Wearing a flowing robe of raccoon skins over his shoulders and strings of pearls around his neck, Powhatan was flanked by his counselors. Behind them sat the potentate's wives and daughters, including Pocahontas. Smith reported that the females wore white feather crowns and necklaces of white beads. Some had also painted their faces and shoulders a bright red.

A great banquet was brought forth for Powhatan, his advisors, and his captive. While they ate, the Indian men discussed Smith's fate at great length. After the feast, Powhatan suddenly ordered his guards to place two blocks of stone, one atop the other, on the ground in front of him. His guards then forced Smith to kneel and lay his cheek on the top block. Encircling the captive, they raised their heavy wooden war clubs high over his head.

Smith was preparing to take his last breath when he felt another body flung across his own. Turning his head as far as he could, he saw that his savior was his young friend, Pocahontas. Just before the clubs fell on both of them, Powhatan called a halt to the execution.

Smith's account of his rescue by Pocahontas is now one of the most repeated tales in American history. Its popularity owes much to Smith's skill as a storyteller. Throughout his life, he displayed a brilliance for taking his experiences and turning them into dramatic tales, with Smith himself always at center stage.

Many 20th-century anthropologists, however, offer a somewhat less romantic interpretation of the events in Powhatan's longhouse. These scholars suggest that Powhatan had probably ordered a mock execution for Smith as a way of making him an honorary member of the Powhatan tribe. Pocahontas may have been part of the staged drama, playing a traditional role as the protector of the adoptee. But whether she was acting on her own initiative or merely acting a predetermined part, Pocahontas's involvement in the ceremony clearly displayed her importance in her father's eyes.

Pocahontas is shown saving Smith from her father's executioners in this illustration from Generall Historie. *Although one of the most popular American legends, Smith's account of this event is probably inaccurate. Many scholars now believe that Powhatan staged a ceremonial mock execution, in which Pocahontas played the role of savior, as a way of adopting Smith into the Powhatan tribes.*

Seemingly against the wishes of Opechancanough and some of the more militant counselors, Powhatan ordered that Smith be released. The chief then began to interrogate the prisoner directly. By Smith's own admission, his answers were all lies, invented to save himself in what appeared to him to be a trial for capital offenses.

Why were the English remaining in Powhatan territory? Powhatan asked. Did they plan to establish a permanent colony? No, replied Smith; their ship had been damaged, and he and the other men were waiting for another English vessel to carry them home. Why had he

King Powhatan comands C: Smith to be slayne, his daughter Pokahontas beggs his life his thankfullness and how he subiected 39 of their kings. reade ẙ history.

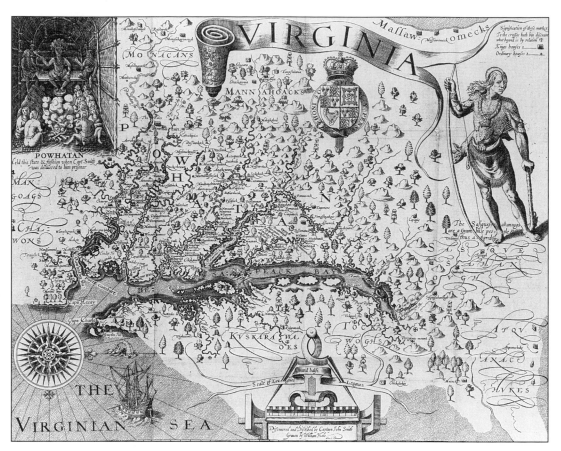

been exploring the area's rivers? To look for "the backe Sea," said Smith, explaining—in partial truth—that they had been sent to look for a route to the Orient.

Powhatan then surprised Smith by proposing a friendly trade: in exchange for English arms, the Powhatans would give the Jamestown settlers much-needed food, such as corn and venison.

Smith quickly agreed, which pleased his captor. According to the Englishman, "with all the kindness [Powhatan] could devise, [he] sought to content me, [and] sent me home with 4 men."

Shortly after Smith safely made his way back to Jamestown, the *Susan Constant* returned as well. Just as Captain Newport had promised, he had loaded the ship

A 1612 map of the portion of Virginia "discovered and described by Captayn John Smith." The vast area in the center labeled "Powhatan" shows the extent of the chief's rule.

with food, tools, and more settlers. Pocahontas was visiting her English friends that day—January 2, 1608—and probably watched nearly 100 men disembark. Among them was a surgeon, a goldsmith, a jeweler, a tobacco pipe maker, and a perfumer.

The expanded work force promised improved fortunes for Jamestown. However, only five days later, a devastating fire swept through the colony. Left in ashes were the church, many of the colonists' homes, and, worst of all, the storehouse full of the food Newport had brought back for the remainder of the winter. Starvation and illness again threatened the colonists.

Upon learning of the disaster, Pocahontas intervened once more. Accompanied by servants bearing what Smith listed as "bread, fish, turkeys, squirrels, deare and other wild beasts," Powhatan's daughter appeared at the Jamestown gate. All through the bleak days of January and February, the colonists looked on in wonder as still more Indian messengers arrived every few days with vast portions of game, fish, and cornbread.

Although he abided his daughter's charity, Powhatan himself was feeling less than generous toward the colonists. Learning of the colony's latest additions, the chief no longer believed Smith's story that Jamestown was only a temporary settlement. Powhatan was sure that the English were planning to slowly increase their numbers in order to take over his realm.

The werowance developed a strategy for eliminating the foreigners. He would continue to barter food for English weapons. Once he had accumulated enough cannons, muskets, and hatchets, the Powhatans would overpower the Englishmen with their own arms.

In order to carry out his plan, Powhatan sent Pocahontas to Jamestown with an invitation for Captain Smith. At the end of February, Smith, Newport, and about 40 colonists were escorted by 200 warriors to Werowocomoco. There, nearly 500 more Powhatans greeted them.

Smith wrote that Powhatan, dressed in finery, "strained himselfe to the utmost of his greatness to entertaine [us] . . . with the most plenty of victualls he could provide." After their feast, Smith presented Powhatan with gifts from England, including a red woolen suit, a white greyhound, and a sugarloaf hat like that favored by King James. Goodwill appeared to abound until Powhatan asked his guests to lay down their arms while in his longhouse. Suspecting that Powhatan had designs on their weapons, Smith refused, but tried to comfort the werowance by promising to help the Powhatans battle their Indian enemies.

Newport was less cautious in dealing with his host. To Smith's irritation, he displayed an array of English knives, hatchets, and scissors before the Indians, offering to trade the items. In the end, Newport exchanged 12 copper kettles for some corn. Even though no weapons had changed hands, Smith felt uncomfortable with his associate's eagerness to deal with Powhatan.

To Smith's dismay, Newport continued to trade with the chief. Soon after the colonists had returned to Jamestown, Powhatan sent messengers carrying 20 turkeys to the fort. Newport reciprocated by sending back 20 swords.

On April 20, 1608, Newport sailed for England, promising once again to return with new recruits and provisions. After he had left, 20 more turkeys were delivered to the colonists. Clearly, Powhatan assumed that the exchange he had established with Newport would continue. Smith, however, had no intention of sending more swords to the man he was beginning to see as Jamestown's worst enemy. The colonists kept the turkeys, but at Smith's insistence sent nothing in return.

Powhatan was furious. If he could not trade for the weapons he wanted, he would simply take them. On his orders, Powhatan warriors began ambushing Jamestown. In one of these skirmishes, Smith captured seven Indians.

In May 1608, Powhatan sent Pocahontas to Jamestown to negotiate for the release of the prisoners. According to one English witness, Anas Todkil, the brave girl asked Smith to "excuse [her father for] the injuries done by some rash and untoward [warriors]." Recognizing his debt to Pocahontas for the many times she had come to the colonists' rescue, Smith relented and released the captives into her care.

Throughout the spring and summer, Pocahontas frequently came to Jamestown. These were not friendly visits as much as diplomatic missions. She was acting as Powhatan's ambassador, bringing the colonists messages from her father as well as food.

Despite her efforts, the relationship between the Powhatans and the English continued to sour. Smith's election as president of the Jamestown council only added to the growing tensions. At every opportunity, he used his new position to intimidate the Indians.

On October 8, 1608, Captain Newport arrived in Jamestown with another shipload of English settlers, food, clothing, and implements. Also on board, designated for Chief Powhatan, was an array of gifts that included two very special items: a coronation robe and a copper crown. Newport had received orders from James I to crown Powhatan as "emperor," a title implying that the Indian leader and his tribesmen were subjects of the English monarch.

The royal order directed Newport and Smith to stage the "coronation" in Jamestown and to be sure that when Powhatan received his crown, he knelt in deference to his new lord, the king of England. This gesture was meant

to signal to the entire Powhatan Confederacy that it now owed allegiance to an unknown ruler who lived somewhere across the great ocean.

Powhatan may not have been schooled in the fine art of European diplomacy, but he had a sophisticated and highly developed sense of politics. He knew that the English, with their talk of coronations and allegiances, were playing a not-so-subtle power game. After receiving word of the English king's wishes, the chief sent Smith his response:

> If your King have sent me presents, I also am a King, and this is my land. . . . Your father [Captain Newport] is to come to me, not I to him, nor yet to your Fort, neither will I bite at such a bait.

Powhatan's message presented Smith and Newport with a dilemma: If they went to the chief, rather than forcing him to come to them, they reduced the dignity of the

A 19th-century depiction of Powhatan's coronation by Captains John Smith and Christopher Newport. James I charged the Englishmen with the task of offering Powhatan a crown and the title "emperor." Although unschooled in English diplomacy, the Indian leader recognized that the "honor" was actually a way of tricking him into kneeling in deference to the English king.

English crown. If, on the other hand, they failed to perform the coronation, they would be defying their king's command. Choosing the lesser of two evils, they packed up the crown and robe and went to Werowocomoco.

Not surprisingly, the coronation turned out to be unimpressive, even farcical. Powhatan agreed to don the red robe, but he flatly refused to kneel while the Englishmen crowned him. Determined to force him to obey their orders, Newport and Smith pushed down on Powhatan's shoulders and jammed the crown on his head. Powhatan could not have felt much pride in the honor bestowed on him by King James. The effort to subjugate him to a foreign monarch irritated him profoundly.

The winter of 1608–9 proved the hardest the colonists had yet endured. Rain had been scant that summer; neither the settlers nor the Indians had been able to harvest enough corn to last through the cold months.

It was in the midst of this horrible period that Smith went to Werowocomoco and asked Powhatan for a large supply of corn. The mistrust Powhatan had developed for the Englishmen following his coronation had only grown in the intervening months. Smith's arrogance in asking for still more aid annoyed Powhatan, but he became furious when the Englishman once again refused to set down his weapons at the chief's request.

The true story behind Pocahontas's rescue of John Smith during his first meeting with her father remains a mystery. But it is known that after this encounter, Powhatan was very sincere in wanting to see the brash captain executed. It is also clear that Pocahontas was not merely playing a role when she raced through the forest to warn Smith of her father's intent. Against her father's wishes, possibly against all logic, she had decided to risk her life of privilege and take a path that left her future far from certain.

G·VEEN

6

THE STARVING TIME

This de Bry engraving appeared in Thomas Hariot's Brief and True Report of the New Found Land of Virginia, *the first illustrated description of the New World published in English. According to Hariot's caption, de Bry's image captures the appearance and dress of a young Indian woman of "good parentage."*

In 1609, Pocahontas had reached a turning point. At 13, she had just come of age in the Powhatan culture. She was no longer thought of as a girl by her people. She was now considered a young woman who would soon need to choose a marriage partner and begin her own family.

But Pocahontas was no ordinary Powhatan adolescent. Already set apart by her position as a member of the royal court, she had also firmly decided that she would not follow the path her society expected her to take. By telling Smith about Powhatan's plans to assassinate him, Pocahontas had not only defied her father but also defied the supreme leader of her people. Although reared as a Powhatan, she had declared that her primary allegiance was to the English.

That year was crucial for Powhatan as well. Like his daughter, he remained curious about the English. Smith in particular interested him. With his unshakable courage and determined attempts to communicate in the Indians' tongue, the captain had singled himself out as the most colorful inhabitant of Jamestown. However, Powhatan realized, Smith was also dangerous. His plot to kill the captain may have been foiled, but Powhatan's resolve to destroy the leader and his colony was as strong as ever.

Powhatan ordered more attacks on Jamestown in the early months of 1609. By the end of the summer, he would launch an all-out campaign against the colonists that they called Powhatan's War.

As president of the Jamestown council, Smith tried to improve the colonists' situation in the face of escalating hostilities. Under his direction, the fort was enlarged and the colony's well was deepened to increase the water supply. Smith also recruited two Powhatan prisoners to assist the settlers in clearing 30 acres outside the fort and planting the plot with beans, corn, and pumpkins.

In July, Smith's work was interrupted by the arrival of a familiar English ship, captained by Samuel Argall. Argall brought some startling news from London. From now on, Jamestown was to be funded by a new company—the Treasurer and Company of Adventurers and Planters of the City of London for the First Colony in Virginia. Headed by Sir Francis Bacon and the earl of Salisbury, the firm was flush with capital to subsidize the struggling colony. It had outfitted seven ships to bring nearly 600 new settlers to Jamestown. The fleet, known as the Third Supply, was due to arrive any day.

Smith breathed a sigh a relief. With the Third Supply's arrival, Jamestown was sure to survive. Then Argall told the captain he had still more news for him. Behind the Third Supply was another fleet of ships. Aboard one of these vessels was Lord De La Warr. The new company, Argall explained, had appointed De La Warr the governor of the colony.

Smith's relief turned to fury. After all his efforts to keep the colony alive, he was being replaced as Jamestown's leader. Smith's reaction was characteristic. He immediately left Jamestown, sailing off in a small boat to see Pocahontas's half brother Parahunt. From him, Smith procured some land where he planned to build a

In 1614, five years after John Smith left Jamestown, he returned to North America to explore New England. This engraving of Smith was published in his Description of New England *in 1616. The portrait was accompanied by a poem, praising its subject for "thy faire discoueries and Fowle Overthrowes / Of Salvages, much Civiliz'd by Thee."*

house for himself. If he could not be president, he refused to have anything more to do with Jamestown.

A run of bad fortune, however, prevented Smith from carrying through his plan to create his colony of one. A bag of gunpowder he was carrying caught fire and blew up, leaving him severely burned. His injuries were so painful that Smith decided to give up the battle of surviving in the wilderness and return to the comforts of England.

Shortly before Smith set sail, a delegation of colonists lodged a series of formal complaints against him. Smith was not an easy man to get along with. While president, he had angered most of the colonists by inflicting harsh punishments on those he deemed were not working hard enough.

The colonists' particular grievances were varied, but many shared the belief that Smith was responsible for their disastrous relations with Powhatan. The strangest and most serious charge against the captain, however, was that he plotted to marry Pocahontas so that he would inherit Powhatan's power. With this accusation, Smith was essentially being charged with treason. If he was, in fact, attempting to become a white werowance, then he was betraying James I by seeking to take command of the region, including the king's colony.

For three weeks, the Jamestown council debated Smith's case. Despite his abrasive manner, Smith still had some loyal friends among the colonists. They organized the captain's defense, in which they emphasized Pocahontas's youth and characterized her relationship with Smith as only that of very dear friends:

> Very oft shee came to our fort, with what shee could get
> for Captaine Smith; that ever loved and used all the
> Countrie well, but her especially he ever much respected:
> and she so well requited it, that when her father intended
> to have surprised him, shee by stealthe in the darke night
> came through the wild woods and told him of it. But her
> marriage could no way have intitled him by any right to
> the kingdome, nor was it ever such a thought; or more
> regarded her . . . than in honest reason.

Smith was found innocent on the charge of treason. He was allowed to leave Jamestown and set sail for England on October 1, 1609, without so much as a good-bye to his young Indian friend.

Soon after his departure, a disturbing rumor circulated through the Powhatans' villages: Captain Smith had died.

The English were possibly responsible for spreading the gossip. George Percy, who was appointed the temporary president of Jamestown, wanted to be sure that Powhatan understood that he would never be dealing with Smith again.

Upon learning of Smith's departure, Powhatan severed all ties to the colonists. Pocahontas was ordered never to go to Jamestown again. Even worse for the English, Powhatan declared war on the colony. The Indians stepped up their raids, each time acquiring more weapons to turn upon the colonists in future attacks.

Worn down by these ambushes and their rapidly diminishing supply of food, the Englishmen grew desperate. In this state of despair, they were thrilled to receive an invitation from Powhatan to visit Werowocomoco. The werowance promised that if they would "bring their ship and sum copper," he would "fraughter [freight] her backe with corn." The Jamestown residents had plenty of reasons to distrust Powhatan. But then again, they thought, maybe like his daughter he had at last taken pity on them and only wished to help.

Wanting to believe in Powhatan's newfound generosity, 62 colonists traveled to Werowocomoco. When they arrived, the massacre began. The Powhatans killed 60 of their visitors and took 1 captive. Only one man was able to escape. He raced back to Jamestown to report the tragedy.

The colonists now knew that they were completely on their own. Neither Pocahontas nor Powhatan would provide them with any more aid. They would have to face the cold winter by themselves with almost no food or supplies.

The winter of 1609–10 proved to be Jamestown's most desperate days. For years after, the colonists remembered the period as "the starving time." Plagued by disease as

well as famine, their population dropped from 490 to 60 in six months. The survivors, many on the verge of dying themselves, buried the dead at night, so the Indians would not learn of their diminishing ranks.

If the colonists thought they were keeping their miserable situation a secret, they were mistaken. Spanish ships regularly sailed up and down the Atlantic coast, and reports on the inland English colony had reached several vessels. In 1610 the Spanish ambassador in London wrote to his king, Philip III,

> The Indians hold the English surrounded in the strong place which they had erected there, having killed the larger part of them. . . . Unless they succour them with some provisions in an English ship . . . [t]hey must have perished before this.

A ship did in fact come to the rescue of the 60 starving colonists. Six of the seven ships of the Third Supply had arrived in Jamestown the previous summer. However, the seventh vessel, the *Sea Venture*, never arrived. On the missing ship were the highest ranking officers of the fleet: Sir Thomas Gates, the governor's deputy; Sir George Somers, admiral in command; and Captain Christopher Newport, the veteran sailor who was making his final transatlantic voyage. As time passed with no word of the *Sea Venture*, the colonists assumed the ship had been destroyed in a storm and that all those aboard were dead.

In fact, the ship had been blown off course by a hurricane in the Bahamas, where the 100 crew members were able to navigate the storm-tossed vessel to the island of Bermuda. For 10 months, they made Bermuda their home while they constructed two new ships, the *Deliverance* and the *Patience*, from the wreckage of the *Sea Venture*.

Finally, the crew was able to set sail for Virginia. When they arrived at Jamestown on May 23, 1610, the exhausted travelers expected to be warmly greeted by the

During Powhatan's War, celebrations such as the one shown in this de Bry engraving were a common sight. Singing and shaking rattles, Powhatan men and women always gathered around a fire after a successful battle.

Lord De La Warr was named the first governor of Jamestown. The appointment was a great challenge. He arrived in Virginia on a ship full of fresh recruits just as the Jamestown settlers, starving and weary, were preparing to give up the colony and return home.

inhabitants of a prosperous colony. Instead, to their shock, they found the dying colonists pathetically huddled in a fortification in ruins. Sir Thomas Gates wrote of the experience: "We found the pallisadoes torne downe, the Ports open, the Gates from off the hinges, and emptie houses (which Owner's death had taken from them) rent up and burnt." Gates and his associates gathered up the sickly survivors and settled them aboard the *Deliverance* and the *Patience.*

On June 7, 1610, Gates ordered that the ships set sail down the James River. The English were giving up and abandoning Jamestown. At last, Powhatan had his empire back.

The two vessels proceeded down the river until night

fell. The crew then anchored them off Mulberry Island, intending to continue their voyage home at dawn. When day broke, several men looking out into the Atlantic saw something amazing. Three English ships were sailing toward them.

Aboard one of the vessels, the *De La Warr*, was the new governor himself. When it reached the river, Lord De La Warr immediately conferred with Gates. The governor was disturbed by the story of the Jamestown survivors. He was possibly equally distressed by their plans to desert the settlement. In England, De La Warr had been excited to receive his prestigious appointment. He had taken great pains to learn about Virginia and its inhabitants, and was not eager to see all of his preparations go to waste.

Taking command, the governor ordered the *Deliverance* and the *Patience* to turn back. The timing of his arrival, he declared, had been a sign. God Himself had willed it. De La Warr swore that he would thereafter be a servant to the Almighty's divine plan. Under his leadership and with the help of the 150 new colonists, Jamestown would be resurrected.

Captain Samuel Argall is shown meeting with the leaders of the Chickahominy tribe in this early-17th-century engraving. Argall was ever eager to deceive the Indians. Posing as Pocahontas's friend, he took enormous advantage of her trusting nature.

Capit. Argal

7

HOSTAGE TO THE ENGLISH

As Lord De La Warr entered Jamestown, he could not have looked more out of place. With the eyes of the ailing settlers upon him, the new governor paraded through the colony wearing a velvet suit decorated with ruffled trim and jeweled ornaments. He was followed by 50 servants, all decked out in crimson-colored jackets. The message was clear: De La Warr intended to bring English civilization back to Jamestown.

The governor's love of luxury and pomp, however, did not prevent him from ruling Jamestown with an iron hand. Supervising the colonists' labor from his private quarters aboard his ship, he immediately implemented a work schedule, in which everyone but him was expected to contribute to the rebuilding of the colony. De La Warr's plans for Jamestown were ambitious. He declared that two new forts would be built at Point Comfort and that a new palisade would be constructed around Jamestown itself. He also wanted more land cleared so that the colony would be able to grow enough crops to feed itself.

The governor was equally determined to deal with the Indians harshly. He refused to accept Powhatan's ban on trade with the English, even though virtually every tribe throughout the confederacy was complying with their leader's proclamation. Lord De La Warr sent a simple message to Powhatan: Trade with us or face the consequences. According to the governor, the chief replied "that either we should depart this country, or confine ourselves to Jamestown only." If the colonists did not respect Powhatan's wishes, "he would give a command to his people to kill us, and do unto us all that mischief which they at their pleasure could."

Although the threat of Powhatan's power was still keenly felt by the colonists, few Englishmen had seen the chief in years. Ever since the day he had ordered Smith's execution in January 1609, Powhatan had shuttled between two villages, Orapaks and Rassawrack, located deep in the Virginia forest to the north of Jamestown.

Pocahontas had also retreated from sight. Soon after her father ordered the massacre of 60 colonists in the fall of 1609, she left Powhatan's court, traveling 90 miles to the north to take up residence with the Patawomeke (Potomac) tribe. Powhatan's violent campaign against the English had convinced Pocahontas that she could no longer live with her strong-willed father.

Her break with Powhatan was not complete, however. Among the Patawomekes, she acted as the chief's tribute collector. The populous and prosperous Patawomekes were part of the Powhatan Confederacy. Yet the tribe lived far enough away from Powhatan's sphere of influence to enjoy a certain amount of autonomy. Seeking her own independence, Pocahontas must have relished living with people who felt free to do as they pleased without the constant interference of her powerful father.

While Pocahontas dwelled with the Patawomekes, reports that she had married began to make their way back to Jamestown. According to these rumors, her husband was a Patawomeke warrior named Kocoum. Virtually nothing is known about their union, not even whether the marriage actually ever took place.

The next record of Pocahontas's activities comes from a young Englishman named Henry Spelman. Spelman had been part of an exchange program that had been set up when Smith was the leader of Jamestown. To foster goodwill between the Indians and the colonists, Spelman and two other English youths, Thomas Savage and a boy named Samuel, went to live among the Powhatans; in turn, two young Powhatan Indians arrived in Jamestown.

In the early fall of 1610, while Spelman was living in Rassawrack, Pocahontas and Pasptanze (the werowance of the Patawomekes) came to the village to visit Powhatan and possibly to give him the tribute his daughter had collected. By this time, Spelman was eager to return to his own people, and the visitors seemed to offer a means of escaping from Powhatan's realm. As Spelman later wrote, "the King of [the Patawomekes] . . . shewed such kindness to Savage, Samuell, and myself, as we determine to goe away with him."

When Pocahontas and Pasptanze left Rassawrack, the three boys secretly followed them. Just outside the village, however, Savage, who was a great favorite of Powhatan's, began to have second thoughts about their escape. According to Spelman, "Having gone a mile or too on the way, Savage fayned some excuse to stay and unbeknownst to us went back to the Powhatan and acquainted him with our departing with yc Papawomeke."

Upon learning of the boys' unannounced departure, Powhatan became furious. He sent a party of warriors out to track them down. When the warriors found them, they ordered the English youths to return to Rassawrack. Spelman and Samuel both refused and ran off, with the search party in close pursuit. One of the warriors caught up with Samuel and killed the boy with an ax. The horrified Spelman raced away deep into the woods.

By the time the youth had escaped his pursuers, he was completely lost. He would probably have perished in the forest if not for Pocahontas, who discovered Spelman and took him with her back to the Patawomekes. Pasptanze offered Spelman sanctuary, and the young Englishman stayed in the village for several weeks.

In September 1610, the Patawomekes had another English visitor. Samuel Argall, who had been captaining the *De La Warr* when it brought the governor to Jamestown, arrived among the tribe after losing his way while trying to sail to Bermuda. Argall was happy to meet Pasptanze, especially when he learned the werowance was willing to trade with the English despite Powhatan's ban. The captain was even more pleased to see that Spelman was still alive. But perhaps most exciting to Argall was his discovery of Pocahontas's whereabouts.

With her accustomed kindness, Powhatan's daughter warmly welcomed the wayward captain. In this case, however, her good heart would work against her. Argall saw in Pocahontas not a good friend but a means of helping the English expand their land holdings in the region. He reasoned that if the English took Pocahontas hostage, they would have a great advantage over Powhatan. The chief might not abandon his war in order to save his daughter, but he would certainly be more willing to negotiate with the English if Pocahontas's fate was in their hands. Argall soon left the Patawomekes without attempting to implement his plot to kidnap Pocahontas. But in the years to come, the idea was never far from the captain's mind.

The next spring, Jamestown saw still another change in leadership. Despite his privileged accommodations, De La Warr fell ill, forcing him to return to England in March 1611. He left behind a colony that was somewhat rejuvenated but hardly prosperous.

Sir Thomas Dale came to Jamestown in May 1611 to serve as the settlement's military commander. Feeling that past commanders had been ineffectual, Dale was determined to rule with an iron hand. He immediately imposed martial law on the colonists in an attempt to make them work harder.

Two months later, a new marshal and deputy governor of Jamestown arrived on Virginia's shores. Sir Thomas Dale, an experienced military man, found that without a harsh leader forcing them to work, the Jamestown settlers were languishing once again. Dale immediately imposed martial law on the colony. The death penalty was to be enforced for a variety of offenses, including deserting the colony, robbing from its food stores, and displaying disrespect for the English king.

Like De La Warr, Dale had great plans for Jamestown. He intended to build four new forts along the James River to protect the colony from the Powhatans' attacks. Even more ambitious, Dale announced that he would found a new English settlement, Henrico, named for King James's oldest son, Henry. It was to be located on an elevated peninsula about 45 miles upriver from Jamestown, an easily defensible site personally chosen by Dale.

The establishment of Henrico was a tribute to Dale's leadership. Under his command, the lazy colonists constructed an elaborate and secure outpost. Ralph Hamor, the colony's secretary, left this firsthand description:

> There is in the town three streets of well framed houses, a hansome Church, and the foundations of a more stately one laid of Brick, in length an hundred foote, and fifty foot wide, besides store houses, watch-houses, and such like . . . upon the verge of the river, five fair Block houses wherein live the honester sort of people . . . and there keep continuall centinall for the townes security.

In founding Henrico, Dale also meant to send a message to Powhatan—the English were not only staying, they were growing in numbers and expanding their territory. In a letter to Lord Salisbury in London, Dale plainly stated his intentions regarding the chief: "I should so overmaster the subtle, mischievous Great Powhatan that I should leave him no room in his country to harbor in, or draw him to a firm association with ourselves."

The population of the two English settlements grew substantially when, in the summer of 1612, six tall ships arrived with 300 men aboard, among them Sir Thomas Gates, who had been named the new governor of Virginia. The recruits, as additions to the colony's labor force, were certainly welcome. However, finding the provisions to feed these men seemed an almost impossible task.

Remembering his old friends the Patawomekes, Captain Argall came up with a simple solution. After traveling up the Potomac River, he renewed his acquaintance with Pasptanze and succeeded in persuading the werowance to trade with him. In March 1613, just when the granaries at Jamestown and Henrico were nearly depleted, Argall returned to the colony with 1,100 bushels of corn.

During this trip to the Patawomekes, Argall finally set his plot to kidnap Pocahontas in motion. Possibly he had been ordered to abduct her by Gates or Dale, but in any case, Argall himself was enthusiastic about his mission. He wrote, while setting sail for his trip up the Potomac, that he vowed "to possess myself of her by any strategem that I could use."

To help capture Pocahontas, he enlisted the assistance of two Patawomeke friends, a man named Iapassus and his wife. At first they were reluctant to be a party to the kidnapping. But after Argall promised to give them a copper kettle, all their scruples disappeared.

According to Argall's plan, Iapassus and his wife invited Pocahontas to visit the Englishmen's ship, the *Treasurer*, one evening. She gladly accepted the invitation as she was, in Argall's words, "desirous to renue her familiarities with the English." Once she was aboard, Argall took her for a tour of the ship, then entertained her at dinner.

After the meal, Iapassus suggested that Pocahontas rest before returning to the village. The Patawomeke couple

escorted her to the gunners' room, promising to come back soon. They shut and locked the door, picked up their kettle, and sailed away.

In the dark room, Pocahontas sat silently. All around she heard muffled English voices. She listened closely but, knowing only a few words of their language, could not make out what was being said. Then, suddenly, the door opened and Argall entered. He announced that she was a prisoner of the English.

The *Treasurer* set sail for Jamestown. Three years had passed since Pocahontas had last seen the settlement. Even though just a girl, she had then marched proudly through the colony, flanked by servants carrying baskets of corn for her foreign friends. But now, as the ship anchored and she was led ashore, Pocahontas walked

A 17th-century engraving of Pocahontas's abduction by Captain Samuel Argall. To the right, Argall's two co-conspirators, an Indian man named Iapassus and his wife, are extending to Pocahontas an invitation from the captain to come aboard his ship. During her visit, she was locked below deck as the ship set sail for Jamestown.

slowly with her eyes to the ground, attended only by English soldiers determined not to let her escape.

As soon as Argall had delivered his hostage to Gates, an Indian messenger bearing a ransom note was sent to Powhatan. The note explained that Pocahontas would be released only after the chief returned all the English captives he held and the tools and weapons he had stolen. The English also demanded a large supply of corn. Hamor recorded Powhatan's reaction:

> This unwelcome newes much troubled Powhatan, because hee loved both his daughter and our commodities well, yet it was three months after (not, that is, until July) ere hee returned us any answer: Then . . . he returned seven of our men, with each of them an unserviceable Musket, and sent us word, that when wee would deliver his daughter, hee would make us satisfaction for all injuries done us and give us five hundred bushels of corne, and for ever be friends with us.

The colonists realized that Powhatan would never meet all their demands. As much as he loved Pocahontas, he knew that he did not have to worry about the English harming her. She was a prize too valuable to mistreat. Also, to the class-conscious English, Pocahontas was considered royalty, and therefore she had to be treated with the utmost respect.

Her care was entrusted to Alexander Whitaker, a young, well-educated minister with an uncommonly high opinion of his Indian neighbors. In a 1613 sermon, Whitaker explained to his parish that the Indians "have reasonable soules and intellectuall faculties as well as wee; we all have Adam for our common parent."

Living on Whitaker's 100-acre farm near Henrico, Pocahontas had to adapt to an entirely new way of life. Years before, she had delighted in learning about English culture. Now, however, she was having the colonists' customs thrust upon her. Once an amused observer,

Pocahontas, as a hostage, was being forced to give up her identity as Powhatan's privileged daughter and become an English lady.

The first step in her indoctrination was to change her appearance and manner. Her short doeskin skirt was taken away and replaced with a tight-fitting whalebone corset, a long-sleeved blouse, and an ankle-length skirt. Dressed in her new clothing, she was taught to walk with her head bowed modestly through the dust-covered streets of Henrico.

Whitaker's next task was to instruct Pocahontas in the tenets of Christianity. According to all existing accounts,

An engraving entitled Baptism of Pocahontas, *based on a 19th-century painting that now hangs in the U.S. Capitol in Washington, D.C.*

she was a willing and eager student. These chronicles, however, were written by colonists, who desperately wanted to prove to the Crown that they were fulfilling their mission to save Indian souls.

After years of war, famine, and disease, the settlers were thrilled to announce that they had at last found their first native convert. Only weeks after her abduction, Dale wrote the bishop of London in triumph:

> Powhatans daughter I caused to be carefully instructed in Christian religion, who after shee had made some good progresses therein, renounced publickly her countrey Idolatry, openly confessed her Christian faith, was, as she desired, baptised.

With her baptism, Pocahontas not only lost her own religion; she also had to forsake her name. From then on, she was known as Rebecca. To the English, Pocahontas had ceased to exist.

Ætatis suæ 21. Aº. 1616.

8

LADY REBECCA

What shoulde I doe," John Rolfe wrote to his friend Sir Thomas Dale in 1614. Rolfe had a unique problem, one that had never been faced by an Englishman before: he had fallen in love with an Indian woman, the now 18-year-old Pocahontas.

Pocahontas's admirer had come to Virginia accompanied by his wife in June 1609. Traveling on the *Sea Venture*, they and the other passengers had been shipwrecked off the coast of Bermuda and spent the winter on the island. During that time, Rolfe's wife gave birth to a girl, whom the couple named Bermuda after their temporary sanctuary. Either on the island or on the trip from there to Virginia, both Rolfe's wife and the infant died.

In Virginia, the young widower took a great interest in cultivating tobacco (or the "esteemed weed," as he called it). The Indians of the region had long grown a variety of the tobacco plant, *Nicotiana rustica*. After curing the plant with herbs, oils, sumac leaves, and dogwood bark, they smoked the leaves. For the most part, the colonists stayed away from this tobacco. Smoking it burned the tongue and scratched the throat and nose, sensations they found entirely unpleasant.

However, another type of tobacco, *Nicotiana tabacum*, was more to their liking. This plant was grown by the Spanish on plantations in colonies they had established in the West Indies. In a short time, the tobacco proved to be a lucrative export crop for Spain. It was so lucrative, in fact, that it produced more income than all the Spanish gold and silver mines in the Americas.

Through some unknown means, Rolfe was able to procure a few seeds of this precious plant. In 1611 or 1612, he began cultivating a crop in the sandy soil between the James and York rivers. The plant quickly took root and flourished in Rolfe's Tidewater fields. His success as a tobacco grower was a tremendous boon to the economy of the colony and of England.

A 1626 engraving of Powhatan farmers harvesting a crop of tobacco. Colonist John Rolfe had tremendous success as a tobacco grower. His exportation of tobacco to Europe brought much-needed funds into the English colony in Virginia.

Sometime in 1613, Rolfe journeyed to Henrico to scout for more fertile land. A devout Christian, he probably met Pocahontas at one of Reverend Whitaker's services. In any case, the Indian chief's daughter and the English gentleman became fast friends.

Months later, writing to Dale, Rolfe revealed the depth of his emotions in his loving descriptions of "Pokanhuntas to whom my harties and best thoughts are, and have for a long time been so intangled, and inthralled in so intricate a laborinth." Still, the Englishman was hesitant to marry his beloved. Even though Pocahontas was a Christian convert, Rolfe confessed to Dale that he was worried about the impropriety of marrying a woman who had been born a "heathen."

Dale, however, wholeheartedly approved of the match. In his estimation, the union between a prominent English colonist and Powhatan's daughter could only be advantageous. Pocahontas's conversion had already been a feather in Dale's cap. Likewise, he might be able to use her marriage to Rolfe to show the colony's financial backers in London that he was dealing successfully with the Indian menace.

With Dale's support, Rolfe asked Pocahontas to marry him, and she accepted his proposal. But before the wedding, Dale decided that still another person should be consulted about the matter—Powhatan. The English had not heard from the chief in several months. Aside from his initial gesture of returning seven hostages and a few old, battered weapons, he had made no response to the English ransom demands.

In March 1614, Dale, Rolfe, Pocahontas, and 150 other colonists sailed to Werowocomoco, which Powhatan had reestablished as his home village. They anchored in Poetan Bay, only a few miles away from the settlement. Their arrival was surely acknowledged by the Indians, but the chief made no attempt to greet the travelers.

After several days, some Powhatan warriors approached the ship. Dale told them that the purpose of their visit was to "deliver up the daughter of Powhatan and receive the promised return of men and arms." The Indians responded with a halfhearted attack from the shore. Dale then ordered the colonists to disembark and set fire to a few of the Indians' houses. After this minor conflict, a truce was declared.

Powhatan then was willing to make a gesture. He sent two of Pocahontas's brothers to the ship, ordering them to bring back a report on their sister's welfare. Pocahontas told her kin that she was upset by her father's refusal to negotiate for her release. She further explained that her captors had treated her considerately and declared that she wanted to continue to live with the English.

In the meantime, Rolfe and another colonist, John Sparks, went ashore to seek out Powhatan. His tribespeople led them to one of the chief's spokesmen. Powhatan considered speaking with them a breach of protocol; he would only meet with their leader, Dale.

By messenger, Rolfe informed Powhatan of his intention to marry Pocahontas. The chief surprised him with his reaction: Powhatan not only approved of the union but also agreed to end his war with the English. Now in his late seventies or early eighties, the great leader of the Powhatan Confederacy declared that he was tired of fighting.

On April 5, 1614, Pocahontas and John Rolfe were married. The ceremony took place in the church at Jamestown. Pocahontas wore a "tunic of Dacca muslin, a flowing veil and long robe of rich material" imported from England. Around her neck was a string of glittering freshwater pearls, a wedding present from her father. Pocahontas's uncle Opitchapan and two of her brothers were in attendance, but the mighty Powhatan declined

In March 1614, Pocahontas—accompanied by Dale, Rolfe, and 150 other colonists—arrived in Werowocomoco, seeing her father's village for the first time since her kidnapping. Powhatan would not meet with her, but sent two of Pocahontas's brothers in his place. Pocahontas's anger at this slight and at Powhatan's refusal pay her ransom was evident. She told her brothers that she had decided to remain among the English.

his invitation. He probably feared that an appearance at Jamestown might be read by the English as a sign of surrender.

Powhatan, however, did bestow a generous gift on the wedding couple—a choice parcel of land about 40 miles north of Jamestown along the James River. There Pocahontas and her new husband built a house, naming it Varina, after the Spanish word for the variety of tobacco Rolfe had so successfully introduced to Virginia.

Soon after the wedding, Dale sent Ralph Hamor to pay a call on Powhatan at Werowocomoco. On Dale's behalf, Hamor asked Powhatan if Dale could have the hand of the chief's youngest daughter in marriage. Powhatan refused, explaining that the young woman was already due to wed a neighboring werowance.

But the chief had his own question for Hamor: he wanted to know how Pocahontas and Rolfe "lived, loved, and liked." The colonist replied that Powhatan's daughter was "contented" and had no intention of returning to live among her own people. According to Hamor, Powhatan then laughed and asked him to take a message back to Dale: "There have been too many of his men and mine slaine, and by my occasion there shall never be more . . . for I am now olde and would gladly end my daies in peace."

Powhatan's words did not put a halt to all of the fighting between the Indians and English, however. There were still minor skirmishes, but on the whole the two groups briefly became more tolerant of one another. This new era was named the Peace of Pocahontas.

In 1615, Pocahontas gave birth to a son christened Thomas, probably after Sir Thomas Dale. Jamestown's financial backers awarded the infant and his mother an

A fanciful 19th-century depiction of the wedding of Pocahontas and John Rolfe. Their marriage ushered in the Peace of Pocahontas, a period of eight years during which the Indians and colonists of Virginia ceased warring.

annual stipend in appreciation for her generosity to the colonists over the years.

At about the same time, the financiers began to collect funds to establish a Christian school for English and Indian children in Virginia. They envisioned Pocahontas, the first Indian convert, as an ideal spokesperson for their fund-raising project. "She will goe into England with mee," Sir Thomas Dale wrote to the bishop of London. Dignified, intelligent, and now quite conversant in English, Pocahontas, Dale concluded, could easily persuade businessmen, the clergy, and maybe even royalty to invest in the colony.

In the spring of 1616, when Pocahontas was about 20 years old, she set sail for England on the *Treasurer*, the same ship on which she had been abducted three years earlier. Accompanying her were her son, husband, and about a dozen Powhatan men and women. When they arrived in England, Pocahontas and her entourage caused an immediate sensation. The English were impressed by Pocahontas's regal appearance and struck by the exoticism of her Indian companions. They were especially fascinated by one tribesman, Tomocomo. Dressed in a short leather breechcloth, he had painted both his face and body and had pulled back his hair with a stuffed snake and the skin of a weasel.

A confidant of Powhatan, Tomocomo was instructed by the chief to count every Englishman he saw. He abandoned his assignment soon after his arrival. Later reporting to Powhatan, Tomocomo asserted that the people of England numbered as many "as the stars in the sky, the sand on the English beaches, or the leaves on the trees."

Pocahontas and her Powhatan traveling companions were surely stunned by the size and wonders of 17th-century London. During their trip, they saw London

Bridge, Westminster Abbey, and St. Paul's Cathedral. But the highlight was a visit to the king's palace.

Captain John Smith was responsible for Pocahontas's royal invitation. An old associate of the Virginia Company asked Smith to write a letter to Queen Anne, the wife of King James, recommending that Pocahontas be presented to the court. Obligingly, Smith wrote of the many times that Pocahontas had come to his and his countrymen's aid during the early years of Jamestown. Without the Indian woman, he maintained, the English would now have no colony in Virginia.

A Long View of London, engraved in 1616, the year Pocahontas visited England. She was surprised by the city's size and population. Before her trip, she knew only the English settlements of Virginia, which were small and unimpressive in comparison with the Powhatans' own villages.

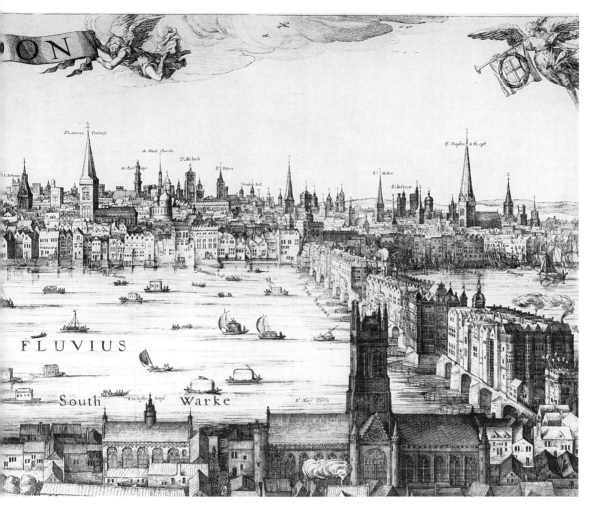

Queen Anne was sufficiently impressed. She invited Pocahontas to her court and asked Lord and Lady De La Warr to attend the Indian woman. To commemorate the event, the Virginia Company commissioned an official portrait of their now celebrated visitor. In the painting, Pocahontas looks like a true English noblewoman, wearing a dress of brocaded velvet and a wide lace collar.

Pocahontas made her court appearance in Whitehall Palace, a splendid royal residence overlooking the Thames River. A former Jamestown settler, Robert Beverley, chronicled the event: "[Pocahontas] behaved her self with so much Decency, and show'd so much grandure in her Deportment, that she made good the brightest part of the character Capt. Smith had given of her."

After several weeks of attending court functions, Pocahontas began to feel ill, seemingly suffering from a respiratory ailment. To aid her recuperation, the Rolfes traveled to Brentford, a small town with a drier climate located nine miles west of London. Soon after settling in at the Brentford Inn, they received an unexpected visitor—John Smith.

Eight years had passed since the two had last met. Upon seeing Smith alive and well, Pocahontas was at first so stunned she could not speak. She rose, excused herself, and left her quarters. Several hours later, she returned and sat down to have a conversation with her long-lost friend.

In a slightly recriminating tone, she explained that the English "did tell us alwais you were dead." Pocahontas added, however, that the Powhatans never quite believed the rumor. In fact, her father had asked Tomocomo to inquire about Smith "because your countriemen will lie much."

According to Smith, Pocahontas referred to him as "father" throughout their visit. When he asked her why, she replied, "You did promise Powhatan what was yours should bee his, and he the like to you, you called him father being in his land a stranger, and by the same reason so must I doe." After a brief exchange, the two parted cordially, never to see one another again.

In February 1617, the Rolfes began to prepare for their return to Virginia. They booked passage on the *George*, a ship captained by Pocahontas's former captor, Samuel Argall, but were detained when fierce winds prohibited it from sailing. Finally, in the second week of March, the bad weather subsided and the passengers were allowed to board. By now, however, Pocahontas was extremely ill. She was lying down below deck as the ship journeyed down the Thames toward the Atlantic Ocean.

About 25 miles outside of London, Argall gave orders for the ship to dock at the town of Gravesend. Pocahontas, too sick to continue, was carried ashore to a nearby inn. John Rolfe was grief stricken. Attempting to console him, his wife said "all men must die," adding while pointing toward young Thomas, "'tis enough that the childe liveth." Shortly after, Pocahontas died. Her remains were buried at St. George's Parish Church along the banks of the Thames.

De Bry's sensational depiction of the Powhatans' 1622 massacre of 300 colonists, which ended the Peace of Pocahontas. The English countered the Indians' attack with a vicious campaign to annihilate the native peoples of Virginia.

This statue of Pocahontas stands at her gravesite in the yard of St. George's Church in Gravesend, England. It is a replica of a monument to Pocahontas erected in the 1900s near the entrance of the Jamestown National Historical Site in Virginia. Today, many of the state's most distinguished families claim the Indian woman as an ancestor.

Leaving his son behind in England in the care of a friend, Rolfe continued on to Virginia. Upon his arrival, he sent a message to Powhatan, informing the old chief of his daughter's death. Soon after, Powhatan passed his supreme power to his brother Opitchapan and went to live among the Patawomekes as Pocahontas had done years before. A little more than a year later, he died as well.

Opitchapan and his brother Opechancanough assured the English that they would continue to respect Powhatan's peace. But in 1622, the goodwill between the two groups was irrevocably shattered. The militant Opechancanough ordered the killing of 300 colonists. At about this time, John Rolfe's death was reported, but it is unclear whether he perished in the massacre or by some other means.

Thirteen years later, 20-year-old Thomas Rolfe returned to his homeland. His powerful grandfather had willed him thousands of acres of land, as well as his mother's wedding present and his own birthplace, the plantation named Varina. Marrying an Englishwoman, Jane Poythress, he settled there and raised a family. Descendants of the Rolfes are today among the most distinguished families of Virginia. Proudly citing their lineage, they are the living legacy of Pocahontas, the Indian "princess" who devoted her short life to promoting peace among the greatest of adversaries.

CHRONOLOGY

FURTHER READING

Barbour, Philip L. *Pocahontas and Her World*. Boston: Houghton Mifflin, 1969.

D'Aulaire, Ingri. *Pocahontas*. New York: Doubleday, 1989.

Donnell Susan. *Pocahontas*. New York: Berkley, 1991.

Feest, Christian F. *The Powhatan Tribes*. New York: Chelsea House, 1990.

Harris, Aurand. *Pocahontas*. New Orleans: Anchorage, 1961.

Rountree, Helen C. *Pocahontas's People: The Powhatan Indians of Virginia Through Four Centuries*. Norman: University of Oklahoma Press, 1990.

————. *The Powhatan Indians of Virginia: Their Traditional Culture*. Norman: University of Oklahoma Press, 1989.

Smith, John. *Captain John Smith's History of Virginia: A Selection*. Indianapolis: Bobbs-Merrill, 1970.

Wood, Peter H., et al., eds. *Powhatan's Mantle: Indians in the Colonial Southeast*. Lincoln: University of Nebraska Press, 1989.

Woodward, Grace S. *Pocahontas*. Norman: University of Oklahoma Press, 1980.

INDEX

PICTURE CREDITS

ANNE HOLLER has worked as an archaeologist in New England and lower Manhattan and has taught art and anthropology at Hunter College in New York City. She has also written articles on history and archaeology for the *New York Times.*

W. DAVID BAIRD is the Howard A. White Professor of History at Pepperdine University in Malibu, California. He holds a Ph.D. from the University of Oklahoma and was formerly on the faculty of history at the University of Arkansas, Fayetteville, and Oklahoma State University. He has served as president of both the Western History Association, a professional organization, and Phi Alpha Theta, the international honor society for students of history. Dr. Baird is also the author of *The Quapaw Indians: A History of the Downstream People* and *Peter Pitchlynn: Chief of the Choctaws* and the editor of *A Creek Warrior of the Confederacy: The Autobiography of Chief G. W. Grayson.*